Build Your Wealth Through Property Investment

The Essential Buy to Let Property Investment Strategies for UK Investors

Charles Fletcher

© **Copyright 2022 - All rights reserved.**

The content contained within this book may not be reproduced, duplicated or transmitted without direct written permission from the author or the publisher.

Under no circumstances will any blame or legal responsibility be held against the publisher, or author, for any damages, reparation, or monetary loss due to the information contained within this book, either directly or indirectly.

Legal Notice:

This book is copyright protected. It is only for personal use. You cannot amend, distribute, sell, use, quote or paraphrase any part, or the content within this book, without the consent of the author or publisher.

Disclaimer Notice:

Please note the information contained within this document is for educational and entertainment purposes only. All effort has been executed to present accurate, up to date, reliable, complete information. No warranties of any kind are declared or implied. Readers acknowledge that the author is not engaged in the rendering of legal, financial, medical or professional advice. The content within this book has been derived from various sources. Please consult a licensed professional before attempting any techniques outlined in this book.

By reading this document, the reader agrees that under no circumstances is the author responsible for any losses, direct or indirect, that are incurred as a result of the use of the information contained within this document, including, but not limited to, errors, omissions, or inaccuracies.

Table of Contents

INTRODUCTION 1

CHAPTER 1: UNDERSTANDING BUY TO LET 3
    Overview of a Buy to Let 3
    Why You Should Invest in a Buy to Let 5
    Things to Consider in a Buy to Let Investment 6
    The Future of Buy to Let 9

CHAPTER 2: GETTING STARTED IN YOUR BUY TO LET JOURNEY 13
    What Investing In a Buy to Let Involves 14
    Working Out the Initial Research 17
    Buying a Property 22

CHAPTER 3: BUYING THE RIGHT BUY TO LET 25
    Buy to Let Property Checklist 25
    Types of Buy to Lets 31

CHAPTER 4: MANAGING YOUR BUY TO LET 37
    Understanding Your Role as a Landlord 37
    Basic Property Management 41
    Working Out Costs 45
    Legal Requirements and Certifications 47

CHAPTER 5: TAX IMPLICATIONS AND REGULATIONS 53
    Keeping Up With the Tax Rules 53
    Calculating Tax for Buy to Let 55
    Mortgaging the Buy to Let 60

CHAPTER 6: BUYING NEW OR REFURBISHING 65
    Buy to Let and The City 65
    Pros and Cons of HMOs 70
    Renovating and Refurbishing a Buy to Let 73
    The Pros of New Builds 76

Work Checklist and Cost 78

CHAPTER 7: WORKING OUT THE FINANCIALS 83

RETURN ON INVESTMENT 83
THE DEMAND FOR BUY TO LETS 86
TOUGHER RESTRICTIONS ON FINANCING 87

CHAPTER 8: BUILDING YOUR BUY TO LET PORTFOLIO 91

BUY TO LET PORTFOLIO CHECKLIST 94
COVER ANY PITFALLS 99

CONCLUSION 103

REFERENCES 105

Introduction

Whether you have been living in the UK all your life or have emigrated to the country only a few years ago, you would no doubt have come across the term "buy to let." You may not have wondered too much about it till you started living on your own as a tenant somewhere, so you would need to get as much information as possible. However, most tenants only have a few standard questions before they start living in rental spaces. All they need to know is what the rent is, when it's due, and whether or not the place has heating.

Once you venture into becoming a landlord yourself, i.e. owning property for the purpose of renting out, you should know all the questions that can come up. Prospective tenants will want to know more about what the accommodation will provide for the price, such as maintenance and internet connectivity, who the property will be managed by, what the policy on pets is like, what the provisions for parking and storage are, and if there are any concerns with the neighbors, to name a few.

Some might even ask if it is called a buy to let or a buy-to-let, and it is safe to say that you have also asked yourself this question at one point. More importantly, you should also be well-versed in the type of tenancy agreement you will be entering with any prospective tenants, which is why it is important for you to know as much as you need to in order to create confidence.

My property investing career began where I was born, in Surrey. Now, I live in London and I own developments in the metropolitan area. I've been in the property industry for many years selling across London and Surrey, and have also done developments. You could say that it's the family business, as my family have been buying and selling, as well as working on property developments, for just as long as I have.

My reason for writing property books is this: I love property and teaching people how to attain success through property investment. There isn't a single "right" strategy for anyone. The beauty of property investing is that you can implement any number of methods and achieve success. With success comes financial freedom, and this has been my motivation towards becoming an author who specializes in and loves the property field.

After all, that's why we're in this, aren't we? The promise of financial freedom is a huge incentive for us to do whatever it takes to be successful. I'm here to help you along your path and show you how property investment can take you there. In my books, you're going to find details on the strategies that have helped me in the past which have contributed to the rapid growth of my portfolio.

With *Build Your Wealth Through Property Investment: The Essential Buy to Let Property Investment Strategies for UK Investor*s, you will learn how you can make a mark in the lucrative world of buy to lets, how you can make them work for you, and the common pitfalls that you will need to avoid. If you think you don't have enough money to make them work, think again. With this book, I will show you how you can leverage a small amount of money to create a large amount of wealth, as well as a happy and satisfied customer base.

Chapter 1:

Understanding Buy to Let

Overview of a Buy to Let

To begin with, a buy to let is a property purchased for the purpose of being rented out, or "let" out, to prospective tenants. Oftentimes, buy-t0-let properties are residential, including flats and house shares located in the city center. Buy to lets are ideal for prospective tenants who are unable to afford their own property due to the rising cost of property prices everywhere, particularly in urban locations close to the city centers. Thus, tenants prefer renting a living space that is closer to their workplaces as well as other urban amenities such as shopping areas, offices, schools, restaurants, and more, and are connected with a robust public transportation system.

Buy to let, or BTL, properties can be owned by individual property owners or by smaller or larger companies that are looking to create a reliable revenue stream. Their primary tenants are people unable to purchase a property of their own due to various challenges; the most obvious being the price barrier for anyone without the means. The "generation next" that referred to people being born from the 1970s to the early 2000s has now become the "generation rent" due to skyrocketing prices of everything from commodities to real estate. The cost of living has been on a steady rise which doesn't equate with the salaries and revenue streams for full-time and part-time employees. This makes it challenging for most millennials to get on the property ladder, even for an entry level property, and it won't be before they retire and draw a pension that they can consider buying a house.

These properties are located conveniently near city centers which have led to higher rents. Nevertheless, people prefer renting out a buy to let either by themselves or as a house share, i.e. two or more people sharing a house together and splitting the rent. In June 2022, the online property portal Rightmove PLC reported that average asking prices for properties in the UK had risen by £55,000 since before the COVID-19 pandemic (Rightmove PLC, 2022). According to a report published by Statista Research Department, the biggest rental demographic in the UK in 2020 ranged between the ages of 25 to 34 years, which comes to 1.4 million private renters (Statista, 2022).

The proximity to workplaces is a major deciding factor when it comes to choosing a property to rent, as it means shorter commute times and economical fares. In some cases, tenants can find a place that is within walking distance to their workplace, which either provides a good deal of savings or offsets a higher rent. If they stay at their job for the long-term, they may not move out, even if they do get another place at a much lower rent.

Another viable option of renting out buy to lets is the concept of houses in multiple occupation, or HMOs. As the name suggests, HMOs allow landlords to rent out a property to three or more people who are not of one household, or family, and will have their own living space within the property, i.e.

bedrooms. However, the tenants will be sharing common spaces such as living rooms, bathrooms, kitchens, and gardens. This is commonly referred to as a house share. This is an ideal option for students and professionals who are breaking out on their own and have a limited budget for accommodation, as they can effectively pool in the rent of the property to the landlord.

Why You Should Invest in a Buy to Let

Based on the trends of modern millennial preferences for living in rented accommodations, it is no wonder that investing in buy to let properties is a tremendous opportunity if you are looking to have passive income. Both tenants and landlords have various benefits when it comes to entering such an agreement, and as a prospective landlord yourself, you need to know about both if you want to make the most of your experience.

First, evaluate the type of accommodation you are looking to provide depending on the needs of the prospective tenants. When you plan on investing in a property, it would have to be an ideal location for whoever it is that will be staying there. More than likely, your prospective tenants will either be natives or people from abroad looking to settle in somewhere close to the city that is in a reasonable proximity to their place of work. The same goes for students and their place of learning, such as universities. Managing the property is another concern, especially if you are looking to invest in a buy to let for passive income. If you are not available at all times to look after the property and deal with the tenants' concerns, you could hire a property manager for this purpose. Estate agents also offer this service, however, there is a cost attached to this which could offset your whole investment.

Next, of course, is the financial gain you have to make out of a buy to let property. The goal here is to let your property work and earn for you. As a landlord, your property can make you a regular monthly income in the form of rentals that can be used to pay for the residential property's mortgage, maintenance, renovation, repair due to wear-and-tear, and any other existing debt on the property. Naturally, this income can also factor in a profit for yourself considering you are offering a service, i.e. your property to a tenant. Therefore, the rent pricing has to take all of the above expenses into account.

Aside from the monthly income from the rent, owning a buy to let property is also a sound long-term investment. According to the Office for National Statistics, the property prices in the UK have seen an increase of over 50% in the last 10 years. The average property price has gone from around £170,000 in June 2011 to £278,000 in March 2022. The latter price is a £24,000 increase from the same time only a year prior (Lewis, 2022). Any landlord with a buy to let property in 2011 is in a good position to sell off the asset and be able to pay off any debts while also collecting a sizable profit if they see fit, else they could continue collecting on the monthly rental payments. However, whether it is a buy to let or any other kind of residential property, it will be subject to Capital Gains Tax. It is important to look over the government guidelines as this tax varies depending on the person and property.

Things to Consider in a Buy to Let Investment

On the surface, investing in a buy to let is appealing as it provides guaranteed returns on your property as long as you have the right kind of financing available. However, things don't always stay the same, and buy to lets—like most real estate investments—come with their own set of challenges. For one thing, there is a constant change in interest rates which tend to go up rather than down. In June 2022 alone, the Bank of England increased the base interest rate to 1.25% from 1%. This results in knock-on effects for all kinds of property owners, buy to lets included, especially those who have variable and tracker mortgages. While mortgage lenders can set the interest rate in a variable mortgage, a tracker mortgage is bound by the rate set by the Bank of England. In the case of tracker mortgages, the amount of interest that borrowers have to repay increases along with the interest rate, as these mortgages are tracking the rates according to the Bank of England. Most investors with multiple buy to lets will have taken out different loans against these properties, so an increase in the interest rate is likely to affect their repayment targets, thereby affecting any future planned investments such as more buy to lets. It will also affect their ability to take out more loans for new properties considering the increase in interest rates.

Aside from financial considerations, property owners should also understand that people's priorities constantly change. The most recent example is of the pandemic, following which the dynamics of traditional housing requirements have shifted. People who are able to work remotely from home or have the option of a hybrid working system, i.e. part work-from-home, part working on-site, don't necessarily need to bother with the proximity of their home to the workplace or longer commute times. This allows them to choose accommodation located further away from most locations in the city centre with better quality of life and lower rent.

Furthermore, if the concept of hybrid working picks up more steam in the future, these trends can see greater widespread acceptance, making other property locations more appealing for tenants. Not only that, tenants will want to have places with provisions for working from home, such as a home office, garden space for exercise and recreation, faster internet connectivity on wireless networks, closer proximity to parks, public places, cafes, restaurants, and supermarkets, car parking or garage, and the quality and finish of the property itself. In a Homebuyer Wishlist report by Market Financial Solutions, the priorities of residents shifted greatly from 2019 to 2021. While tenants cited the distance to nearby towns or cities as the fourth-most important factor and internet connectivity as eighth in 2019, the situation has become nearly the reverse in 2021 with internet connectivity being third-most important while distance to nearby town or city all the way down to 11th place (Market Financial Solutions, 2022).

This still does leave people who have to be physically present at their workplaces, including essential services such as healthcare, logistics, supply chain, retail, hospitality, transportation, and more. Therefore, consider the kind of tenants you want to attract to go with the property you are looking to rent out, and whether or not their needs synchronize with what you have to offer. Moreover, as the property owner, you will also need to consider the needs of potential buyers when you plan to sell your property off in the future. Regardless of a tenant or a potential buyer, both parties will have their own requirements that need to be fulfilled by the property and all its amenities, ergo it falls on you to ensure that they are getting their money's worth. Understanding what the market is like and staying up-to-date on how people's preferences are constantly shifting from time to time is crucial as a property owner and landlord.

Also, don't forget the longevity of the property itself. This means the property can undergo renovations or refurbishments to make it habitable, improve its life, and enhance the property value. If you decide to rent out a property that is in need of refurbishment or renovation, you won't be expecting a higher rental income. But that can change by performing renovations and refurbishments as and when needed, along with the necessary maintenance. These additional works are bound to make the property more marketable as it will offer enhanced living standards, thus allowing you to charge a premium rental income.

Let's not forget the all important matter of financing a buy to let property, which means securing the best loan before purchasing the property. This will be discussed in greater detail in the following chapters.

The Future of Buy to Let

As mentioned earlier, the dynamics of what tenants want out of a rental property have evolved in a post-pandemic world and how landlords can work on bridging the gap between what they have to offer and what prospective tenants want. With the emphasis on having living spaces with great work-from-home facilities such as a room for a home office and faster internet access, tenants are becoming more and more open to the idea of less expensive properties located in commuter towns or dormitory towns, i.e. communities habited by people who travel from one city to another for work and with no major industries of their own. Aside from cheaper rent, commuter towns also offer more space and better access to public green spaces, which are a stark contrast to the cramped concrete jungles of urban centers.

Since commuter towns let people commute to major cities such as London as and when needed while also allowing better work-from-home facilities, the demand for buy to let properties a little outside the cities has grown. The present trends indicate that people want more value for money in terms of how much living space and quality of life they can get versus decreased commute or travel times. Now, it appears that people can cope with the increased commute or travel times if they are working in a hybrid work model, i.e. part work from home, part at the office, in order to have larger accommodation in a cleaner neighborhood, far away from the hustle and bustle of crowded, and also overcrowded, urban centers. Air pollution saw drastic reductions during the 2020 lockdown immediately after the COVID-19 pandemic, with reductions of up to 30% to 40% in microparticle levels (PM2.5) compared to the same periods from 2015 to 2019 (United Nations, 2021). This reduction in air pollution contributed to an enhanced quality of life for people who found the fresh, pollutant-free air a welcome change. Needless to say, this won't stay the same when urban centers get back to business as usual now that the pandemic days are well behind.

To take the areas surrounding London as an example, there are several small commuter towns outside the capital that are seeing rapid growth despite the distance. The distance can be easily overcome thanks to train travel. Most of these towns offer cheaper rent and a lowered cost of living along with remarkable recreation space. These towns are a great place to invest in for prospective landlords as the demand there is only bound to go up.

An ideal location is St. Albans, Hertfordshire, which is only 21 miles outside London at a 20-minute train ride from St Pancras International. It is also 11 miles away from Luton Airport and the Sunday Times awarded it the title of "the best place to live in the Southeast" in 2020 (Herts Advertiser, 2020). It is a thriving city with shops, markets, schools, transport network, and a sense of history with a grand cathedral and other architecture that harkens back to the Middle Ages. But one of the biggest attractions to St. Albans is the expansive countryside of Hertfordshire with features such as flat walk paths and cycling paths, and quiet but thriving country pubs as well as restaurants. The only downside to anyone moving there from the city is the slow-paced life of the town, with most establishments closing early throughout the week and not many 24-hour conveniences available.

Regardless, St. Albans has registered a continuous growth in the government Rental Index, with figures rising up to 1.3% by June 2021, making it an ideal location for prospective landlords to start investing in. According to Zoopla, a British real estate portal, the average prices of flats in St. Albans stood at £350,417, while the prices for a terraced house stood at £555,632 in June 2021.

Then, there is the town of Royal Tunbridge Wells in Kent, located 31 miles and a 45-minute train journey away from London. It was listed in the Top 10 Happiest Places to Live in Britain in 2018 by Rightmove, a real estate company in the UK, with scenic beauty and ample green spaces surrounding great residential properties. Flats are available at an average price of £322,369, while a terraced house can cost an average £438,107, as per the prices by July 2021. Royal Tunbridge Wells also boasts several restaurants, pubs, and boutique shops making it an idyllic residential community. Similarly, Luton in Bedfordshire also offers closer proximity of just over 29 miles to London and hardly a mile to get to Luton Airport. A 30-minute train journey makes it an ideal location for commuters, however, the rent itself has seen a steady increase of around 30% in the last five years (Office for National Statistics, 2021). This goes to show that Luton has the potential of being a sound investment for landlords. Nevertheless, the cost of housing in Luton still remains very attractive, with flats available at an average price of £153,942 and terraced houses averaging at £232,290. For first-time buyers, it doesn't get any better than Luton.

There are other options further afield with similar railway infrastructure to make commuting more viable. Bedford, Bedfordshire is located 46 miles away from London, but offers a 47-minute commute via train. Further construction of train links will connect the town to Oxford and Cambridge. The prices are also relatively affordable, with flats averaging at £180,680 and terraced houses at £257,309, making it another phenomenal option for first-time investors. Various housing developments have also started mushrooming in Bedford, with some major names in the industry realizing the potential of the town as a commuter haven based on increasing demand. Bedford is also host to the Bedford River Festival, one of most popular outdoor festivals in England that allows free attendance.

Further, further, afield is Peterborough, Cambridgeshire, a historic cathedral city bustling with schools and historical landmarks. The town is situated farther away from London at a distance of 74 miles, but the commute to the capital by train is a swift 48-minutes. The distance also makes the property prices considerably more affordable with flats averaging at £116,740 and terraced houses at £169,247, significantly lower than most of the above towns. There are also plans to expand housing around an area of 166 acres that will accommodate about 1,500 new homes, thus becoming a potential hotbed for buyers and investors alike in the future.

Chapter 2:

Getting Started in Your Buy to Let Journey

As you jump into your life, and ultimately your career, as a landlord, you have to be prepared for both the expected and the unexpected. The more information you have of the issues that can arise in owning and renting out a property, the better prepared you will be to handle a situation, or at least seek out the relevant assistance needed. This involves evaluating the property you are looking to invest in, its long-term viability, its potential rental yield, the kind of neighborhood it is situated in, and how much value it has to offer to the potential tenant. Moreover, there are a host of other legal obligations and pitfalls that require landlords to be on their toes at all times, as they could result in dire consequences. These could be the cancellation of a landlord license or even criminal prosecution simply because a landlord overlooked a certain legal obligation, such as carrying out maintenance and upkeep of a property in order to make it habitable, scheduling safety checks every year, recovering rent from tenants, holding security deposits from tenants, and evicting tenants in case of any violation.

Oftentimes, landlords overlook specific regulations when it comes to buying and renting a buy to let property simply because they feel that the process and obligations will be the same as any other residential property. Landlords would have already had an experience of owning their house from which they must have picked up the basics of managing the property, such as taking care of tax payments and taking out a mortgage. But the rules and regulations for a buy to let property differ from a standard residential or even a commercial property. For one thing, the mortgage itself is referred to as a buy to let mortgage that comprises different rules and regulations. The interest rates are also unique for buy to let mortgages, as is the Stamp Duty.

What Investing In a Buy to Let Involves

The first thing you should do is consult with the necessary advisors for your property, starting with a solicitor; i.e. a conveyancing solicitor. Conveyance solicitors specialize in laws, rules, and procedures regarding residential properties, and are invaluable when it comes to buying and selling residential properties. They take care of the necessary paperwork involved in the transfer of real estate property from one person to another. While it is true that you can go about the process of preparing the paperwork by yourself, hiring an experienced conveyancing solicitor takes a load off your mind. There is a lot more going on in the buy and sale process of a property than taking care of simple paperwork, which is something that most people believe can be taken care of by a landlord. Conveyancing solicitors can expedite the process and also guide landlords through any legal concerns in buying a property and renting it out. Don't forget that conveyancing solicitors offer their services to both buyers and sellers, so whether a landlord is buying or selling a property, the role of the conveyancing solicitor also changes as they deal with their peers among the other parties.

Another important advisor involved in your journey as a landlord is an accountant. Having a good accountant shows that you are very serious in your journey in being a landlord, especially when you plan to expand your buy to let properties for maximum returns. An experienced and skilled account can help landlords to keep their tax liabilities in check, advise landlords on prospective properties and what the market is like for investing or selling, and keep proper accounts that can help landlords gain more funding for growing their portfolio. It's also important to remember that accountants specialize in different areas, which is why you need to evaluate which one would suit your needs more. If they are dealing in real estate, then they should have a healthy stable of property clients and should be able to answer any and all questions that you may have. In ideal circumstances, accountants can also be property investors themselves which provides them the necessary insights on which way the market is shifting. Being involved in the business themselves means that they will be fully aware of the needs and goals of their clients.

Moreover, accountants should also be proactive both personally and professionally. Accountants can have varying personalities, as they could either be outgoing or quiet, but even if they aren't the kind of person who wouldn't mind socializing with you, they should still be proactive when it comes to informing you about how to improve your business and take care of the tax planning without you asking for it. This means prompting you about any industry or market-related issue, any tax changes, and changes in regulations that could have a serious impact on the value of your properties. Rather than you keeping them on their toes, it should actually be the other way around.

Whether it is a conveyancing solicitor or an accountant, it is necessary for you to have a great rapport with them. Naturally, both of them would have a reasonable list of clients which takes up their attention, but being good professionals, they should be able to fit you into their schedule and provide you with a response at the earliest convenience, whether it is a phone message or email. They should also be available to take your calls or get back to you in a timely manner. Most importantly, both solicitors and accountants will have access to your confidential information, which is why there needs to be mutual respect and trust between you. In most cases, getting an accountant or solicitor referred to you by someone you know also lends more credibility, as do any testimonials from other of their clients who you have had a chance to interact with.

That said, there is also the all important matter of pricing. Good advice does not come cheap, and the more experienced and high profile a solicitor or accountant is, the more they are going to cost you. When you set out to invest money in buy to lets, you have to keep track of what margins you will be making and how much of these you can spare for expert help. Opting for a cheaper alternative, i.e. a service provider who does not charge much, may sound fiscally prudent, but can end up costing you money in the short and long-term. Cheaper service providers may either not be very experienced or have a hard time managing their clientele, where they aren't able to coordinate with their clients for managing their portfolio or manage tax planning. There will be a major difference between a less experienced and less expensive service provider and someone who makes your interests a priority, so the rule here is to focus on quality rather than quantity.

With a quality conveyancing solicitor and accountant, you can be sure of getting other benefits. Since it is their job to be involved in the market and knowing who to call in case a situation demands it, you can rest assured that they can get in touch with the right contacts to have the matter sorted. Accountants should have more foresight into the world of the property market and advise you regarding the financial stability of a certain project or property. Their role in being your accountant goes beyond tax-planning and managing the books, although knowing about the tax implications such as the Capital Gains Tax is the primary reason you want them in the first place. Nevertheless, they should be able to provide an in-depth financial review of all your properties and where you can make even more profits, as well as line you up with potential investors who can help you expand your holdings and business scope.

In any event, your advisors should be proficient in their area of expertise and have a strong business acumen and integrity to deliver true value to you as a landlord. Their role shouldn't be limited to filing paperwork or crunching numbers, but should rather be more invested in the welfare and success of your buy to let business. After all, your success ensures their success as well. This is why you should scrutinize your advisers thoroughly and ensure that their credentials and reputation are above board. Also, do your best to get quality people on your team while also keeping the cost in mind so that your profit margins are not affected.

Working Out the Initial Research

Having the right team of advisors on your side is going to aid you in a ton of matters related to your buy to let business, the most important being how to finance the property. Landlords with experience in renting out and acquiring properties have a handle on how to get the right mortgage, but it is not a simple undertaking, especially if you are the kind of person who finds all the different details confusing and overwhelming.

As mentioned earlier, the mortgage you get for a buy to let is going to be different from other residential and commercial properties. Once you apply for a mortgage, you must let the company know that you are going for a buy to let property, in which case they can verify your eligibility for such a mortgage. Ideally, you should do this at the initial stages of your discussion with the mortgage company you plan to go with, as this way, you can find out the mortgage amount that can be lent out.

Furthermore, you will also become aware of the different rules and interest rates that will apply to your property. For one thing, you cannot purchase a buy to let with a regular residential mortgage and then rent the property out. This activity will fall under commercial rental purposes and requires a written authorization from the mortgage company to do so. If you do try to rent out a residential property that has a residential mortgage, you would be in violation of your mortgage agreement's terms and conditions, and the mortgage company would be fully entitled to repossess the property on those grounds.

Then, of course, comes the original problem: money. With mortgage payments due every month, it is always a good idea to have a contingency in case things don't go your way. For instance, your tenant may have problems with paying on time, which means that your regular rental income will see a complete stop altogether. This puts you, the landlord, in a precarious position as you need to cover the mortgage payments. Now, your first instinct may be to become more assertive and even pushy with the tenant, which is not

19

advisable, as it is against the law to harass a tenant for non-payment of rent. It is also possible that your property is between tenants, i.e. vacant, which also ceases any rental income.

This is where having a reserve of funds is important. A reserve is essentially a backup cache of money that you can use to fill in the void of a lack of rental income. Your reserve funds should have at least six months worth of rental income to help you with your mortgage payments and any unexpected repairs or maintenance. Once you do get a tenant, you can then take out a small percentage of your rental yield to cover up the reserve funds and make sure that you have a necessary backup for any unforeseen situations.

Speaking of rental income, your buy to let is going to provide you with an investment yield, i.e. the percentage of income that goes directly in your pocket. While the rest of it will be covering essentials such as managing the property, paying the mortgage, factoring in additional costs such as Stamp Duty, and paying your accountant, lawyer, or estate agent, your yield is why you went into the buy to let business in the first place. Calculating the yield depends on the rent you set for your property against the amount you paid for it. Let's say your property cost you £150,000 to buy and you have set the annual rental at £7,500, making your yield 5% of the original value.

Don't forget that every investment will have its ups and downs. Property investment such as buy to let is no exception, as markets fluctuate and the cost of living varies. The rental you set at the outset of a tenancy agreement is going to be set in store for the duration of the agreement, which can make it difficult for you if there is a major impact on the economy. If the cost of living increases from the time when you get a tenant on board with you, then the rent they are paying may not be sufficient for you to fulfill all your obligations as a landlord. Even if you can, then the obvious casualty will be your own personal profit, or yield, that you rely on to make the buy to let venture a success.

Therefore, always set your rental pricing after discussing it with your accountant so that you can maximize your profit yield while also making sure that your rent is market competitive. Tenants will want the most for their money, so ensuring that you offer a habitable accommodation within a reasonable rent is very important. This way, they will be more than happy to accept any revisions in the rent once the agreement term elapses, as they can expect you to deliver value for money. The better service they get from you as a landlord, the more likely it is that they will continue to stay.

When you set out to acquire your potential buy to let property, you have to look into the current owner and their reputation. It isn't uncommon for existing buy to let landlords to sell off their property to someone else who can continue the same business. Whether you are getting the property from another landlord or a residential owner, you need to make sure that there haven't been any major problems with the property, such as any issues with the wiring, plumbing, fixtures, furnishings, as well as with the neighborhood and security. Be ready to ask questions from the existing property owner, neighbors, estate agents, mortgage companies, conveyance solicitors, and past tenants if you can reach them.

If there are already any tenants renting the property when you are about to acquire it, you need to go over all the details of their tenancy agreement with a solicitor, especially the time the tenancy is about to end. There are procedures in place for new landlords to manage the property and also carry over the existing tenants, however, your solicitor can offer you with detailed legal advice on how to do this. Being a landlord, you may be naturally inclined to allow the existing tenants to enter a new tenancy agreement with you, however, tenants also gain specific rights depending on the nature of their tenancy. If you haven't followed the correct procedures at the time of acquiring the property, it could make it difficult for you to evict the tenants in some cases. Remember that when buying a property from an existing landlord, you are not buying from someone who lives in the property. This means that the seller or existing landlord needs to fulfill certain legal obligations beforehand, like the upkeep of the property. If they have failed to reasonably do so, the responsibility will fall on you as the new property owner and landlord. Granted, the price of the property will fall considerably based on this, but it is far less of a hassle to have a property that is well-maintained than one that needs work and expense before it can be made habitable.

Moreover, if the previous seller or existing landlord is handling all the negotiations themselves without a solicitor, they may not have all the necessary knowledge about the relevant procedures involved and may give you a limited title guarantee. Therefore, make sure that your solicitor is present to make sure that you are protected from any legal concerns that may arise. Also, let your solicitor know of all the background research you have done regarding the property so that they know just as much as you do, if not more, in order to advise you accordingly. This can include any information about where the property is located, how attractive it is for tenants, the current state of the property, the turnaround rate of tenants, the state of its tax payments, whether or not you plan on using an estate agent to manage the property, and more. Also, check the installations and white goods for any warranties and safety certificates, and make sure that they can be transferred to your name, as you will want to have no hassles when it comes to claiming the warranty offerings.

Summing up all your careful research is the matter of price. With fluctuating property markets, negotiating or haggling the price down to what suits you isn't something you should shy away from. This is a standard practice in all property negotiations and there is always room for bringing the price down. You should have a good idea of what prices are like in the neighborhood in order to have a stronger negotiating position. But oftentimes, some sellers may be looking to dispose of the property at a bargain price, which would make you think about why they are so eager. In most cases, it could be due to some financial difficulty they are facing, which is a regrettable situation; in which case, you can exercise your own judgment on whether or not to haggle further. However, this is a business transaction and you have to steel yourself in order to get the best deal.

Buying a Property

Once both parties settle on the price, the next step is to exchange details with each other, such as the name and details of the solicitor. An estate agent handles this for sellers, at a nominal percentage. At this point, nothing is made official and on paper. Neither parties, i.e. the buyer or seller, are in a binding contract yet, which means that you can cancel the deal if the need arises. Depending on your rapport with the seller, doing so under genuine circumstances shouldn't hurt any goodwill, but backing out of a verbal agreement on a whim can impact your reputation in the market and hurt any future possible transactions. Keep your demeanor with the seller pleasant and approachable, and never be rude or arrogant. Always try to keep on excellent terms with all the people involved, including the seller, solicitor, estate agent, and any tenants who are going to revert to you.

To get a mortgage, the first step is to organize a mortgage valuation, or survey, by a qualified surveyor. This is arranged by the mortgage company or lender and usually takes one to two weeks. In some cases, a surveyor does not even need to visit the property for the valuation. This valuation will help the mortgage company verify the value of the property and if it can be used as a security against the loan you are applying for. Mortgage companies provide different survey options, particularly if you are looking to mortgage an older property.

As mentioned earlier, the mortgage for a buy to let property is not going to be the same as a residential property. In some cases, a buy to let property mortgage can be higher than a residential one. This may tempt you to apply for a standard residential mortgage, however, this is strictly not allowed. Any attempts to mislead a mortgage company regarding the type of mortgage you are applying for would be treated as fraud.

Along with a mortgage, you will also need to get specialist insurance that offers coverage for the building itself and the contents within, i.e. the furnishings, fittings, and white goods. This insurance, also referred to as a Landlord Insurance, helps protect you in case of any accident or mishap as a result of the tenant's actions. You should research such specialist insurance for buy to lets thoroughly, as standard residential property insurance will not cover you from any incidents caused by the tenant, such as a fire or damage. If you are getting any Landlord Insurance on cheaper rates, make sure that it sufficiently covers you from any such potential issues. Some specialist insurance also covers your rental income which can help you a great deal if you are paying a mortgage and the tenant is irregular with their payments. Compare different insurance companies and the type of protection they offer, and make the right decision based on what suits your property best after consulting with your accountant and solicitor.

Furthermore, if the buy to let property is going to be your second property (as you may already be owning one as your own house), the Stamp Duty law has changed on second homes. Effective April 2016, you will be paying Stamp Duty on a first home property worth over £125,000 and a second property worth over £40,000. Therefore, the Stamp Duty on a first property worth £125,000 would be 1% while on the other property of the same value, it would be 3%. Depending on what the final price of the property is coming up to during negotiation, you should work out the Stamp Duty and add it to the property cost. This is important to know, as it will affect how you use the income from renting out the property and if you intend to pay the Stamp Duty from the rental income.

Chapter 3:

Buying the Right Buy to Let

Buy to Let Property Checklist

Since the buy to let property is not going to be the place where you will be living personally, your own preferences should not dictate the kind of property you will acquire. This is going to be an accommodation for a certain kind of tenant who has their own needs and expectations. If you put yourself in a prospective tenant's shoes, you would not want to live in a place that has been built or decorated with someone else's tastes in mind. Granted, not every buy to let accommodation can be custom-made to a tenant's exact specifications, but it can get reasonably close to what works for them.

This is why knowing your target market is essential when buying a new property to rent out. The more you know about the kind of tenants you want and the needs they have, the more thorough you can be about what kind of property to get and how it can have maximum appeal to a wider range of tenants through various features and amenities. More often than not, these features and amenities may work for you at some level, but they will be something that the tenants will be after a lot more. For instance, if you are a single employed person, you wouldn't need the kind of space that a family of four would. Similarly, you would prioritize public transport networks if you work a full-time job which could differ from a tenant who works remotely or is self-employed. From the layout to the green space, the decor to the quality of the white goods, your buy to let has to center around the needs of the people who will eventually live there. And even though you cannot predict every single little thing that a prospective tenant will be looking for, you can make sure that you are gearing the property to provide as much as possible to the tenants so that you can have a lot of interested parties.

First and foremost, you have to consider the location of the property and how it conforms with the needs of your ideal tenant. This includes the kind of neighborhood the property is located in, the distance from the city centre, the kind of public transport networks available, and the proximity to essential services such as hospitals or healthcare facilities, schools and colleges, supermarkets, local businesses, greengrocers, public parks, post offices, news agents, gyms, community centers, and more. It is also helpful if the local businesses are offering employment opportunities, which makes it even more attractive for tenants to move into a house and be near to a place of work. These amenities can ensure that you have a healthy pool of potential tenants so that you can rest assured of your property not being vacant for longer periods.

It also goes without saying that safety and security are major priorities for anyone, whether you are a landlord or tenant. Nobody will want to relocate or invest in a neighborhood that has a higher number of crime figures for acts such as street crime and robbery, burglary, trespassing, assault with intent to rob, theft of vehicles, vandalism, sexual assault and harassment, and what-have-you. Moreover, the general demeanor of the locals is also a major factor that can make prospective tenants worried about their safety. Tenants from other regions and countries living on their own could be subject to hate crimes based on race and religion, as well as sexual assault. As a landlord, be sure to get an understanding of the level of security a neighborhood and town has. The most obvious markers are an active police presence and an ethnically and culturally diverse population living in harmony. Towns with an equal concentration of male and female employees in local businesses and institutions makes one feel more comfortable in the knowledge that there is less likelihood of gender-based discrimination or crimes. A reasonable number of places of worship such as churches, temples, mosques, and the like, show that the town is welcoming to and tolerant of people of all faiths.

Closer proximity to universities can attract a pool of students who are always on the lookout for affordable accommodation. You can check the local classifieds or property websites for wanted ads to find out which locations have a shortage of student accommodation. Most students look for places that do not have longer commutes to their university campuses, are available by the start of the term, and have an affordable rent. The cherry on top would be any locations that also have prospective part-time employment available such as waiting tables at a restaurant, working as a check-out clerk at a supermarket, becoming a teaching assistant, or even walking dogs in the neighborhood. In case the rent seems high, students can also live together and pay their share of the rent while also creating a support system for themselves by doing the chores around the house, buying groceries and essentials, and more. Another thing you can look out for is whether a prospective location has a high demand for student accommodation in general but a shortage of appropriate housing. This can create an immediate investment opportunity for you to build a student-housing business.

On the other hand, it doesn't hurt to be located close to the rental property yourself. If you live in the same location or very close to the buy to let, it makes a lot of things easier for you as a landlord. For one thing, you can schedule and conduct viewings for prospective tenants yourself if you live a stone's throw away from the property. This is vital, especially if you are looking for the tenants yourself without the aid of an estate agent. Secondly, it also makes it simpler to manage the property. You can check in with the tenants on a frequent basis at a short drive, address any concerns that they have, and also build connections with electricians, plumbers, and carpenters, among others, who you will need to call upon for any maintenance work.

Then comes the type of building you choose to rent out. Whether it is a flat or a house, an old or new build, or open-floor plans or structured layouts to allow for maximum privacy and storage, each kind of dwelling comes with its own pros and cons. Newer builds do not require a lot of maintenance and have the provisions of upgrading at little cost, making them very appealing to landlords and tenants alike. On the other hand, older builds are more architecturally pleasing and have an old-world charm that a lot of people—particularly the youth—find attractive. Some older builds also have lower rentals compared to newer builds, though this will make both the landlord and tenants question just how fit the place is for living in and whether or not it requires more maintenance.

Newly built blocks of flats are also a preferred avenue for buy to let investment. However, most blocks become saturated with landlords offering the space for rent. As a result, a lot of flats with similar amenities and space become available to tenants who can pick and choose while only considering the difference in price. Newer builds also tend to be overpriced considering the amount of modern amenities they provide, such as more electrical outlets for charging devices, claims of better connectivity to wireless internet, cable TV services, and more.

People also have different preferences for interior layouts. A group of students living in a house share would want separate rooms that afford them some privacy, but would love to have a central communal space including a living room, kitchen, and dining area to gather around in. They may also not have a lot of belongings and have just enough to add a homely touch to the place. Families, however, would want to make roots wherever they live, so they will decorate the place with personal niceties. They would also be living there long-term, which means needing extra storage space, closet space, and more space for activities such as making arts and crafts, studying, playing, and entertaining guests.

Families would also like to have outdoor areas which can foster recreation and relaxation, as well as taking up outdoor hobbies such as gardening. The same could not be said about students or young professionals who will have a lot more on their plate to be concerned with plants and gardens at home. Then again, younger people also prefer having more eco-friendly or green homes, which means eco-friendly construction, renewable energy sources such as solar, proper waste disposal, energy-saving outlets, and smart home technology for a start. And in the age of ride hailing services and a desire to reduce the carbon footprint, most youngsters would forgo parking spaces while people with families tend to have at least one personal four-wheel vehicle. This would make proper parking space and provisions a must-have for the latter.

One aspect of any house or flat that most different kinds of tenants find commonly appealing is the amount of light it gets. Properties with sufficient windows and a bright, spacious atmosphere instantly appeal to people. However, as you survey the property yourself before buying, be sure to look at the property at different times in the day to see how bright it looks and feels. Naturally, the light would look great during the day, but it can start getting gloomy as soon as the sun sets. This would put both the tenants and you off from the property, so make sure that the atmosphere does not turn too dark in the evening, and consider if it looks better with proper electrical lighting.

In order to keep your maintenance costs to a minimum, look out for any signs of damage to the property. This includes leaks, mold, moisture, seepage, rot, cracks, and any structural issues. Not only will this cost you more to maintain, but it could also open you to litigation. You can easily avoid such a scenario by evaluating any obvious damage to the property at the time of purchasing it. Have qualified professionals such as electricians, plumbers, carpenters, and the like, make a comprehensive analysis of the property so that they can advise you on what works well and what needs to be taken care of. At the same time, make sure that all the fittings and fixtures in the house are up to code. This includes electricity and gas connections, water supplies, kitchens, bathrooms, lighting, furniture, and carpeting. It is also important to check the property for any infestations and carry out necessary fumigation and pest control periodically to avoid annoyed tenants.

It's also important to think of where you see yourself with the property in the long-term. Buy to lets are an investment in more ways than one: they provide a passive income as you rent it out, and they should fetch you a tidy sum once you decide to sell it off in the future. If you have done your research about the property and its surrounding neighborhood and town well, you can count on a great resale value potentially to other landlords who are looking to get into the buy to let business.

Depending on how well you have maintained your property, the resale value should be great as long as there are no major problems or disadvantages. The next buyer or potential investor is going to be asking the same questions that you did when you acquired the property, therefore it is imperative that they see business sense in buying it from you.

Types of Buy to Lets

Whether you are looking for a buy to let property in cities such as London, or commuter towns that are easily accessible through the train networks, there are different kinds of buy to lets that you can invest in. It depends on the research you have done about your target market, the pros and cons different properties have, and the budget you have set. Keep in mind that there isn't one perfect kind of property that will suit your goals. All buy to lets cater to a prevailing demand, which means that they are very likely to be a great investment as long as you know what you intend to use the property for. By that, you should remember your target market and their needs. That is a major factor towards having a successful buy to let business with an assured return on investment.

To start off, you can go for standard self-contained flats. As the name suggests, it has everything needed out of an accommodation, such as a bedroom, lounge, kitchen, bathroom, and is secured by a front door, as per UK housing law. A bedsit can also be considered a self-contained flat as it has a bed near cooking facilities, while the bathroom is separated by a door. Similarly, terraced houses with a main front door can have smaller self-contained flats. By this, the house itself should be divided into multiple flats that have their own bedrooms, lounge, kitchen, and bathroom, all secured by the flat's, or portion's, own front door. This will allow the flat to be used by the designated occupant(s) while a communal hall can be used by all the tenants. However, if a terraced house with a single front door has a single kitchen and bathroom to be used by all tenants, then they would not be considered as self-contained flats, even if the bedrooms are secured by their own doors. This is because the house would have multiple occupancy.

Self-contained flats come with great benefits for the tenant, as it offers each tenant occupant privacy and facilities without having to leave the comfort of their small portion. For landlords, self-contained flats work for multiple kinds of tenants such as couples, professionals, families, and single parents, thus offering you with a diverse pool of tenants to choose from. Moreover, you can also provide either furnished or unfurnished accommodation and decide the kind of tenancy you want to offer. An assured tenancy (i.e. a tenancy by which occupants can live out the rest of their lives in the accommodation and also pass it onto their spouse or heirs after their death) can provide you with guaranteed good tenants and reduce the need of looking for new ones frequently. Other tenancy types such as fixed-term tenancy, i.e. lasting for a term of five years, can be renewed at your discretion if you find you are satisfied with the tenants in question.

However, self-contained flats are profitable as long as all the flats within the property are rented out. If any flat isn't rented out for a significant period, it will create a dip in your revenue stream and create a shortage of funds that you calculated to pay for the property, such as mortgage and tax. Furthermore, considering an assured tenancy is all well and good when you have a great rapport with the tenant, but there is no accounting for what their spouse or heirs will be like if and when the tenant passes away. It is also possible that tenants spend a fixed-term tenancy by being on their best behavior in order to earn enough goodwill that will get them an assured tenancy. But even so, offering assured tenancies requires a ton of due diligence on your part, which doesn't necessarily apply to how they are with you. It could be about how they behave at home, whether or not they have any destructive habits such as consumption or substance abuse, or have exhibited any kind of violent tendencies, such as domestic abuse. Evicting a tenant out of an assured tenancy is a time-consuming and stressful process, therefore, be sure to offer one with the benefit of foresight.

Another most sought-after accommodation are student lets. These are buy to lets that are rented out by students as per different types of tenancy. Most times, students share the accommodation with other students under arrangements including joint tenancy and sole tenancy. In a joint tenancy, there is a single tenancy agreement which all students sign. This agreement grants them equal rights, responsibilities, and obligations to pay the rent. On the other hand, a sole tenancy is signed separately by individual students that grants them a specific room in the property. While they would be living with other students, their relationship is communal and has no bearing in terms of rent. Each tenant will be responsible for their own rent. If one student is unable to pay the rent, only that student is evicted while the others carry on living as long as they clear their dues on time.

There is also the possibility of a sole tenancy signed by one student where one student signs a tenancy agreement and then rents out other students. This is called subletting and the other tenants are called lodgers, effectively making the sole tenancy holder a kind of landlord that is present. Of course, this is only if the landlord agrees under a certain arrangement, by which the tenant can drum up other student tenants and save the landlord the hassle. Keep in mind that a single professional would not be able to live in a student let, even if there is a unit vacant.

Most student lets are rented out on fixed-term agreements for up to a year. This provides landlords with a guaranteed income for that period and they can start finding other tenants to occupy the place, assuming the existing students do not stay on. With the knowledge you have of the nearby universities and of how their terms are scheduled, you can calculate when to expect prospective tenants and how long they will stay by the start and end dates of their school terms. You will notice a substantial influx of students after accommodation much before the term starts, as it can be a very busy task if put off for too long. Students from other towns would like to settle in at the earliest so that they can have all their belongings stored if they need to commute to their hometowns for any reason. This way, your property is not left vacant for long.

Fixed-term agreements also help landlords to ease out any difficult tenants without making their disdain for them too obvious. Unless the students are the rowdy sort, most students are very flexible about the kind of accommodation they get considering their budget. As long as they are getting the property as advertised with all the necessary amenities, and the property is perfectly habitable with a responsible landlord who is looking after it, you will find that students make for very pleasant tenants. The only considerations you have to make are that students are on a budget and cannot undertake redecorating or furnishing a property by themselves. This means that the property must be fully furnished. Furthermore, the proximity of the property to the university is a major deciding factor. The accommodation should be at a reasonable distance and easily reachable either by walking, riding a bicycle, or connected with a rapid transport network. Getting such a property is going to cost you more as you get closer to universities and take care of furnishing, which needs to be factored into your budget.

Also, it goes without saying that, but with the high demand for student accommodation, you will be facing a lot of other landlords offering living space. Universities also facilitate students with accommodation either on campus or close to it by hiring private companies, so you will have to be very competitive in your offering and rent. It is also important that student tenants provide a guarantor at the time of signing the tenancy agreement.

Landlords mainly prefer HMOs, as these help them get higher rental payments than other types of properties. Landlords can price the house share in a way that is affordable to potential tenants, while at the same time offering greater returns than those from renting the property out to a single household. Furthermore, house shares also reduce the risk for landlords if any one of the tenants have to withdraw from their tenancy agreement for whatever reason. Till the landlord can get in another tenant to occupy that space, they still have the rent coming in from the other two shares. That said, landlords need to have an HMO license worth around £600, with renewals every five years. Tenants also prefer furnished HMOs, and though unfurnished HMOs are legal, they are not going to be very appealing.

HMOs also have regulations that you need to comply with, such as providing sufficient kitchen and bathroom facilities. These regulations vary based on the area your property is located. There is also a more difficult process of getting an HMO mortgage versus a standard buy to let mortgage.

Cities such as London and other tourist attractions also provide a great opportunity to run a holiday let. Simply put, a holiday let is a property that gives a tenant a place to stay when they are on holiday. To qualify as a holiday let, the property has to be available for at least 30 weeks, or 210 days, a year for guests. Most guests can stay in a holiday let for 30 days, but once their occupation goes past that, they can only stay for a maximum of 155 days, or over 22 weeks.

Holiday lets have to be furnished for obvious reasons, and such properties are specifically classified in the UK and Ireland. Furnished holiday lets also offer tax benefits, however, it isn't easy getting a holiday let status. It depends on whether or not your property has the standard of furnishings that will qualify as hospitable to visiting tourists, availability for bookings, and the rate of bookings that it can potentially receive. If you are mortgaging a holiday let, you can also live in the property yourself for a certain period in a year.

Chapter 4:

Managing Your Buy to Let

Understanding Your Role as a Landlord

The main reason you intended on becoming a landlord is to build a brand new revenue stream and to essentially make a property earn for you. This will both make and cost you money. From the mortgage to the property, to the paint on the walls to the kitchen sink, everything is going to cost money and all of it is going to pass on to you. Now, you may be hoping that once the rental income from the buy to let starts coming in, the property should pay for itself when it comes to maintenance and upkeep. But ultimately, you have to know whether or not you are going to keep up with those expenses. Even when the property is being inhabited by tenants, it is going to see standard wear-and-tear. However, it won't be the tenant's responsibility to pay for such maintenance or renovation—it will be yours. You could certainly include it in the rental you set for the buy to let, but this is where you need to keep the rental affordable enough for the tenant and profitable enough for yourself to more than simply break even.

With the help of your accountant, you can figure out how much you can invest going forward into a buy to let so that you understand the savings advantages as well as the tax benefits you can make out of your property. You can also draw up a list of things that need to be taken care of in a property before you rent it out and the estimated costs of those items. In order to make the property more appealing and marketable, you should consider a top-down renovation or refurbishment—if it hasn't been done already—including wall paint, tile, electrical and gas fixtures, plumbing, drainage, bathroom, kitchen, and more. You will have to ensure that the electrical wiring is safe, the boiler is running smoothly, the ventilation is working properly, and the plumbing is not leaking. If there is a defective boiler that needs replacing, it will be the landlord who has to replace it, not the tenant. Furthermore, you also have to ensure the safety of the property so that it doesn't endanger the tenants in any way. For this, you will have to take care of any fire hazards, ensure proper emergency exits, repair any damp patches, and arrange an annual CP12 gas safety check via a registered gas plumber.

You can also charge a premium if you are offering a furnished property that includes at least one bed, a sofa, a dining table with some chairs, drapes and carpets, white kitchen items such as a refrigerator or freezer and a dishwasher, and a cooker or stove. As a landlord, you are entitled to collect a security deposit from the tenant to protect a furnished property and all the assets it contains, however, the deposit itself is to be collected in a government-approved tenancy deposit protection (TDP) scheme. This ensures that the deposit is held by a neutral party, i.e. the scheme provider, in case there is a dispute between you and the tenant.

More than likely, buying a buy to let property is going to take you further afield from where you presently live. As we reviewed in the first chapter, the most attractive buy to lets are in commuter towns that exist at a good distance from urban centers but are easily accessible through commuter transport networks such as trains. Nevertheless, don't forget that you won't be living in that buy to let property yourself, which means that you won't have regular access to the property in order to manage it yourself. You could get an estate agent to manage the property, but there is an obvious cost involved considering that you are hiring a third party to mind the property for you. This could be anywhere between 6% to 15% of the rental, depending on whether you hire them for full management services or not. Therefore, if you plan on managing the property yourself, remotely as it were, then you have to be easily reachable to your tenants if anything goes wrong. Make a trip to the property every fortnight and let your tenants interact with you over messaging apps tied to your phone number. This way, your tenants can even send you any pictures or videos of any problems on the property just to make sure that it needs immediate attention.

The long-term viability of your buy to let property also depends on the type of tenant you have staying there and the quality of your relationship with them. This should be a consideration from the moment people start coming over to have a look at your property. Depending on the area where you have the property, your tenants could be anyone from single working professionals, families with children, university students, single parents, tenants receiving housing benefits, and even your own extended family or relatives. You can then equip your property to cater to the needs of the specific tenants you plan to rent out to, such as what fixtures they will need, how much space your property can offer, and also work out the rent according to their financial position.

Identifying your target market, or tenant, starts indirectly from when you are looking at different buy to let properties to acquire. You should start by buying a property in a location that will attract the kind of tenant you are hoping to get. If your tenants are working in the city and need something cheaper and away from the hustle and bustle of the metropolis, then a commuter town is the way to go. If the tenants are students, then they would want to be in close proximity to their universities. Prospective tenants with families will want to know more about the neighborhood such as the nearby schools, daycare services, and availability of household items, while younger tenants would like a location that can offer them an excitable social life such as cinemas, theaters, restaurants, pubs, and much more.

When you do finalize the target market, you can then set about the task of finding tenants by advertising online or going to an estate agent. However, do note that finding tenants is solely your responsibility and does require some work such as scrutinizing prospective tenants, getting their background information, developing rapport with them, finding out more about their needs, getting references, and asking for any financial information. Estate agents can also spread the word about your buy to let and provide you with prospective tenants, for a commission.

As mentioned earlier, you could be acquiring a buy to let property that already has tenants in it. Ideally, it would suit you to keep those tenants once their existing tenancy agreement expires. First, you will need to review what the existing agreement stipulates and how they were being treated by the previous landlord, in both positive and negative aspects. This will help you figure out how to go about catering to these tenants for the short-term if not the long-term and set expectations for how the relationship will continue. If things go well till the time of the agreement's expiry, your tenants may be happy enough with you to consider signing another agreement. However, this is when you will have to set your own terms with them which do not necessarily have to vary from the previous agreement. Either way, you should review a new agreement with your solicitor and estate agent first so that you can get the most out of it.

Finally, be very thorough with the written tenancy agreement. Use a solicitor to ensure that all the stipulations are clearly stated and in no way create any potential hazards for you in the long run. Some landlords attempt to rush through the process or cut corners by getting the agreement prepared by an inexperienced solicitor. In some cases, landlords don't even get a written agreement signed and instead proceed in good faith. This could lead to disaster, as tenants may inadvertently get rights neither of you would have expected. Therefore, always have the agreement and the necessary paperwork prepared through a professional legal representative. Moreover, make sure that the security deposit is stored in a government-approved Tenancy Deposit Scheme.

Basic Property Management

Managing a buy to let property on your own is a lot of work. With an estate agent, you can have certain assurances that they will look after the smooth running of your property and take care of any issues that the tenants may report. But even though estate agents manage properties full-time, you have to consider just how many more they are doing simultaneously, and whether or not they can give yours the same kind of attention. This is why it is better to manage things by yourself, however, there is only so much you can do, especially if your idea behind becoming a landlord was to gain passive income.

As a landlord, you are the first person responsible for property management. This, ergo, makes you the property manager, and it involves various services such as showing vacant units to prospective tenants, organizing walk-throughs, researching the market needs, finding new tenants through classified ads and property websites, maintaining tenancy agreements, collecting the rent, and carrying out any maintenance work—both minor and major—by soliciting professional technicians. You will also have to ensure that the activities within the property are above board by implementing house rules for the tenants so that they do not carry out any sort of offensive or criminal activity. Should the need arise, the landlord will also be responsible if there are any court cases against them by the tenants due to severe dissatisfaction with the property.

In order to be successful as a property manager, you have to ingrain the concept of customer centricity and satisfaction in your mind. The success of your buy to let enterprise depends on how well you treat your customers, i.e. tenants, and how your dedication to them will result in greater customer confidence, positive word-of-mouth, and loyalty. Conversely, a lack of delivery as a property manager can result in decreased revenue, frequent vacancies in your property, and a negative word-of-mouth which can kill any prospects of potential new tenants. Therefore, not only should you develop a great rapport with your tenants, but also focus on how well you can deliver on the promises you made at the time of signing the tenancy agreement.

This rapport-building begins the moment you make first contact with the then prospective tenants who, based on your friendliness and people's skills, could become confirmed tenants. Some of the core principles are valuing their opinions, listening to their concerns, answering their questions in detail or getting back to them with an answer, being proactive about

43

following up with the next steps, and taking a genuine interest in their welfare and interests. Even if they do not end up being your tenants in the short-term, they should still remember you and rely on your advice later on. Who knows, they may end up finishing a tenancy agreement somewhere else and return to you or refer some other people.

Ideally, tenants will want you to be available and ready to listen to their concerns, and provide them with reasonable assurances that you will get to the problem at your earliest. How well they believe in those assurances will then rely on how quickly you expedite their resolution. You can make an excellent first impression at the initial viewing and walk-through of the property by having the place cleaned up beforehand, being personally available to walk them through, answering all their questions about the property, letting them know of any renovation or redecoration work that has been done, and offering coffee and tea with some light snacks. The more involved you are at the first viewing, the more prospective tenants will feel at ease in knowing that you will be just as available afterwards, and you can reinforce this by letting them have your contact details.

Aside from that, you will also need to advertise vacancies through newspaper classifieds and property websites, answer queries from applicants over the phone or email, maintain a list of applicants and conduct a screening process, handle maintenance needs, and also any unfortunate instances of evicting tenants if they violate their agreement or don't pay rent on time. It is also important to have sound judgment skills when it comes to the quality of tenants, as you don't want anyone staying on your property who will not have any regard for it. Though tenants aren't as heavily invested in a property as the landlord is, it is still their dwelling and therefore tenants have an ethical responsibility to look after the house as much as they can. Instead, some tenants can be very callous towards rented properties by frequently damaging furnishings, not cleaning up after themselves, creating infestations of pests, and being generally unfriendly to the landlord and neighbors alike. The quality of tenants also affects the word-of-mouth your property receives and any negative publicity will keep good, decent tenants far away from you.

To complement your role as a landlord and property manager, you also need to have great communication skills. You will be needing these on a regular basis as you interact with tenants, applicants, technicians, contractors, accountants, solicitors, estate agents, and even other landlords and property managers. Your communication should be clear, strong, and to the point whether it is in person, over the phone, or in writing when you have to issue notices to tenants. You should also be well-organized, knowledgeable, and prompt by managing tenants' and applicants' lists, answering queries over the phone or in person, getting quotations from contractors for repairs, keeping spreadsheets of expenses, and following up with your accountant and solicitor over any important matters. Being tech-savvy with the latest apps, such as instant messaging, spreadsheets, and online property portals, will help you to stay up-to-date regarding your business. You will find that going digital will make things a lot easier for you to manage.

Another important quality in landlords is being empathetic. This applies not just to the needs your tenants have of the property but any circumstances that are beyond their control. Tenants could have money problems that may make it difficult for them to pay the rent on time. They may ask for some extra time until they can get the necessary funds. It doesn't take much research to find out if they have a genuine issue or not. It could be due to an illness in the family, an unexpected incident such as a mugging or an accident, or the tenant could be between jobs. This is where you should be prepared to show some flexibility and let them have a reasonable enough time to fulfill their commitment to you. After all, you are running a business and have your own expenses related to the property to fulfill. You could use your reserve funds to manage any shortfall maybe once, but try not to let it become a recurring habit. In such circumstances, be patient and understanding with your tenants, but don't forget to be stern if they do not make payments within the extra time you give them.

It also doesn't hurt to know about things that you normally hire other people for. This includes basic maintenance knowledge such as working a boiler, checking out any white goods for faults, and identifying any leaks in the water piping, among others. Having this knowledge can help you either take care of any immediate concerns right away or contact the relevant person to handle it for you. Other than maintenance, you should also have some knowledge about legislation, including knowledge related to housing, safety, and health. Tenants may not know who to get in touch with, so they will approach you first. Even if you aren't completely sure what to do, you can get in touch with the relevant people who do know about such legislative knowledge.

Working Out Costs

Though your buy to let is going to bring in money, it will also cost you money as well. This is in the form of mortgage repayments, maintenance costs, certifications and licenses, legal costs, and fees paid out to agents, contractors, accountants, and solicitors. It also becomes problematic when you have no tenants. Therefore, you need to chart out the expenses you will incur throughout your tenure as a landlord. You could do this easily with a spreadsheet app on a phone or computer, where you list down the inflows and outflows of your revenue stream.

One of the biggest expenses will be the mortgage repayments. When buying a property, a mortgage company will require a 25% deposit of the property price. In order to repay the mortgage, your rent will have to be set at 125% to 150% of the monthly mortgage amount. A lot of mortgage companies set this as a condition at the time of buying the property. The details of how mortgage companies finance your buy to let investment will be discussed in further chapters.

With the mortgage agreement settled, your next major expense will be preparing the property for welcoming tenants. This means carrying out redecoration, repairs, maintenance, and, if necessary, full renovation. People believe that a full renovation will cost a lot more than repairs and maintenance, however, it turns out that carrying out individual repairs and maintenance can end up costing more than you expect. It's important to get a complete overview of all the repairs required on a property to ask for a proper quote from the relevant contractors, as taking care of everything together can end up costing you comparatively less.

You should also check the area of your buy to let to see if it requires a landlord license. If the local area council has made it mandatory, then you cannot rent out any buy to lets without said license. This can be obtained with a fee and requires you to have the property up to the required safety standards, such as having a gas safety certificate, an electrical installation condition report (EICR), a copy of the tenancy agreement, and landlord insurance. A landlord license is valid for five years and there is no standard fee; usually ranging from £370 to £1000 per property. Tenants can also check up on your landlord license by contacting the councils. Any landlord found without a license or not abiding by the rules could be penalized up to £30,000 for each offence, as well as an order to repay the rent to their tenants for up to 12 months (UK Landlord Tax, 2020).

Also, don't forget to get landlord insurance. While you will need building insurance for the mortgage, landlord insurance provides you with coverage for legal expenses and damages caused by tenants, whether it is accidental, deliberate, or malicious. It also covers loss of rent.

Legal Requirements and Certifications

Aside from the above, there are several hidden and unexpected costs that are involved in making a buy to let ready for business. This requires keeping your property up to safety standards and regularly carrying out maintenance and repairs. Furthermore, you will also need to be very stringent about paying all dues such as the mortgage, taxes, and the service charges for your consultants, including your accountant, estate agents, and legal representatives.

To show that your property is meeting the necessary safety standards, you will have to get the relevant certifications that most landlords don't account for in the very beginning. But factoring in the costs for these certifications will help you have a clear budget and schedule for where and when those payments will be due. One such certificate is the Energy Performance Certificate (EPC). This certificate tells people how energy efficient your property is and is required before you can start viewings with prospective tenants. It means a lot to tenants, as they are concerned about how environmentally friendly the property is, plus it also offers recommendations to make the property more efficient, leading to lower bills in the long run.

EPCs cost between £60 and £120 depending on the property size, location, and type. To take a hypothetical situation, getting an EPC for a one-bedroom flat in a commuter town would cost a lot less than a large house in the city. This cost also covers a survey by an accredited Domestic Energy Assessor. EPCs have been a legal requirement for properties since 2007, which means that your property should already have one if it hasn't been renewed. These certificates are also legally mandatory for renting out the property, though it doesn't apply to listed buildings (HomeOwners Alliance, 2022).

EPCs also have different ratings for properties from A to G, with A being the most efficient and G being the worst. This is important, as any properties with an F or G rating are prohibited from being rented out. Moreover, an EPC is required for when you want to sell the property preferably before it goes on the market. A lower rating on the EPC impacts the property's resale value and marketability. Ultimately, you cannot legally rent out a property with an F or G rating. The only way to improve the rating to E and above is to pay for it. There is a government-set limit of £3,500 that you can spend on improving the efficiency level and rating. This limit is inclusive of VAT. Keep in mind that you won't need to spend all of that amount if you can manage to get your property to an E rating. However, if the overall cost goes above the stipulated limit to get the property to an E rating, you can do as much as possible within that limit and then register for an exemption. A list of valid exemptions are listed on the relevant government website. As an existing standard, if your property does not meet the required rating, you could face a penalty of up to £4,000.

To get an EPC, you can either apply for it yourself or get an estate agent to do it for you. Following that, a domestic energy assessor will survey the property for about an hour, where they will check the walls, roof, windows, boiler, and insulation. Based on the survey, the assessor will provide an estimated cost to heat and power the property which will be present in the EPC. You can also ask for a digital copy of the EPC by email which will make it easier for you to display to any prospective tenants and the estate agent.

Then, there is the Electrical Installation Condition Report (EICR), which certifies how safe the electrical wiring and installations are in the property. Landlords are required to get the electrical installations inspected by a registered electrician, who will provide a report to the landlord. This report should also be shared with the tenants. The electricians will inspect all the electrical installations including the wiring, sockets, switches, fuse boxes, light fittings, extractor fans, and electric showers, if any. This inspection will mostly be of fixtures and therefore won't cover appliances such as white goods, toasters, kettles, and TVs. Nevertheless, a good landlord can ask for a portable appliance test (PAT), even though it isn't a legal requirement. Asking for one just shows that you want to be thorough.

The purpose of this inspection is to identify any hazards that can be repaired, and the same electrician can carry it out at the earliest before they can sign off on the report. This way, you can be assured that the property does not have any hazards. Once the inspection is completed, the landlord will be given the EICR. Such an inspection needs to be done every five years. Tenants will ask for a copy of the report before they move in or are viewing the property, so the report should have been issued within five years. Landlords are required to provide this report within four weeks of being requested. As this requirement is effective from July 1, 2020, you should have gotten the necessary inspection completed and the report by no later than April 1, 2021 (Shelter England, 2021).

The report can either verify that all installations are up to the safety standards or recommend the necessary repair work, along with the date of the next inspection. The report has different codes if it requires further work. These codes are F1, meaning that further investigation is required, C1 for immediate repairs as the installations are dangerous and should not be used continuously, C2 for repairs as it is a potentially dangerous installation, and C3 for improvements needed, though not mandatory as the installation has passed the safety check. Landlords must rectify the concerns on any report with codes F1, C2, or C1 within four weeks or as early as specified in the report. Once the work is completed, you will have to inform the tenant and the council of the same—in writing—within four weeks.

Depending on the size of your property, an EICR can cost anywhere between £125 to £300. This price does not include the cost of electricians and repairs. Alternatively, you can also get an Electrical Installation Certificate (EIC) if the property was rewired or built in the last five years. With an EIC, you won't need to get a safety inspection.

You will also need a gas safety certificate from a registered gas engineer. This certifies that all your gas appliances and pipes are safe and efficient, with no risk of any gas leaks. Any fault in your gas installations could result in carbon monoxide poisoning or explosions, so this inspection must be done every year. The engineer will check appliances such as the oven, boiler, chimneys, and flues, making sure that the appliances are set properly and suited for the room they are located in, are properly connected to the gas pipeline and getting a proper gas supply, and that there is sufficient ventilation for any harmful gases to be vented out.

Much like the other safety certificates and reports, you must provide the tenants with a copy of the gas safety certificate within 28 days of the inspection, either online or on paper. The certificate contains details such as the address of the inspection, the landlord's address, the list of the tested appliances and their location, the date of the inspection, and the result. It also highlights any potential issues and how they can be rectified. The inspection must be carried out by a registered Gas Safe engineer or else it will not be considered legal. The certificate will cost you anywhere between £35 and £90, depending on the number of appliances and the extent of your gas pipe system. In the same vein, smoke and carbon monoxide alarms are a legal requirement for all buy to let properties, though they are not going to be too expensive.

Chapter 5:

Tax Implications and Regulations

Keeping Up With the Tax Rules

Think about what happened when you decided to throw your hat into the buy to let ring and you told the people you knew about it. How was their reaction? Did they sound encouraging? Or were they concerned about how well you would, or wouldn't, do in the business? Did they try to scare you off with any number of horror stories about how the property market is a risky business?

If so, you are not alone. A lot of potential buy to let investors have tried getting into the business but have washed out for one reason or another. For one thing, it is a long-term investment and requires a lot of your time, especially if you are going to manage the property yourself. Apart from that, putting money in a buy to let isn't without its risks. You should only consider doing it if you have the necessary financial resources. This way, you can manage the buy-to-let expenses if there are any unforeseen circumstances, such as any accidental damage to the property that isn't covered by the insurance.

It also doesn't help that the government rules on rental properties keep changing. In the last five years, there has been The Renters Reform Bill, the addition of a 20% tax credit for covering mortgage interest, the increase in interest rates and availability of environmentally-friendly mortgages, and updates to the rules on energy efficiency. You need to be on top of the different rules so that your time as a landlord is relatively hassle-free.

Firstly, if the buy to let property is going to be your second property, as you may already be owning one as your own house, the Stamp Duty law has changed on second homes. Effective April 2016, you will be paying Stamp Duty surcharge on a first home property worth over £125,000 and a second property worth over £40,000. Therefore, the Stamp Duty surcharge on a first property worth £125,000 would be 1%, while on the other property of the same value, it would be 3% on the whole property.

Depending on what the final price of the property is coming up to during negotiation, you should work out the surcharge and add it to the property cost. This is important to know, as it will affect how you use the income from renting out the property and if you intend to pay the Stamp Duty from the rental income. Keep in mind that this surcharge will be in addition to the standard Stamp Duty rates. Also, the above surcharge is applicable to properties in England, Wales, and Northern Ireland, but it is an additional 4% in Scotland for second homes, instead of 3%.

If that weren't enough, there have been other tax changes. Prior to April 2020, landlords were able to deduct mortgage payments from the rental income while calculating tax liability.

This was referred to as the mortgage interest tax relief. Now, landlords are required to pay income tax on the entire rental income regardless of the amount of the mortgage interest. On the plus side, landlords get a 20% tax credit on the interest amount. But any landlords paying 40% to 45% income tax will be subject to paying much more.

Calculating Tax for Buy to Let

If you are getting an annual rental income of £12,000, the mortgage interest payment will come to £4,800 per year. That's £400 per month on a monthly rental of £1,000, if you are paying tax at 40%, whereas if you are paying tax at 20%, it will come to £2,400. This is without taking any other expenses into consideration that could be set against tax. Based on the current tax credit rules, you can get a tax credit of 20% on £4,800 of £960. That will bring your tax bill to £1,440 if you are a basic-rate taxpayer, while for a higher-rate taxpayer, it will be £3,840.

Now, if the previous tax rules were still in effect, it wouldn't matter which tax bracket a landlord was in, as both kinds of landlords could deduct the mortgage payments before calculating the tax. Therefore, landlords could deduct £4,800 from the £12,000 rental income and collect £7,200. While the basic-rate taxpayer paid the same amount as they did now, i.e. £1,440, the higher-rate taxpayer could pay £2,880 instead of £3,840 that they do now. All of these figures have to be declared on tax returns.

One way to cut costs on paying extra tax on rental income is by registering your own limited company to purchase the buy to let property. With a limited company, you can deduct all the expenses of the buy to let as a business expense. This includes the mortgage repayments. Furthermore, as a limited company, you need to pay 19% as corporation tax. This makes sense if you are a higher-rate taxpayer, as you won't have to pay the 28% capital gains tax as per the tax bracket. You can draw the income as dividends with the first £2,000 being tax-free for the tax year of 2022–23. However, you will have to pay tax on any further withdrawals as a basic-rate taxpayer at 8.75%, and at 33.75% for the higher-rate tax bracket. For additional-rate taxpayers, i.e. an income tax of 50% for incomes over £150,000 is at 39.35%.

With a limited company purchasing and owning a buy to let, you have the luxury of withdrawing the rental revenue whenever you need it. For instance, if you have taken some unpaid leave from your regular work—or a sabbatical—you can withdraw the money for that particular tax year to meet your expenses. One drawback is that the limited company will be required to pay corporation tax if there is a profit on the sale of a property. This is referred to as a Capital Gains Tax, i.e. the tax paid on the profit you make on selling any non-inventory asset, including properties, precious metals, stocks, and bonds.

If you set out to sell a buy to let property when the time is right, it is virtually impossible to completely avoid Capital Gains Tax (CGT). Nevertheless, your goal of selling the property is to make a tidy profit, which is why there are ways to minimize the CGT amount at the time of sale. The most important thing to remember is what the rules are pertaining to capital gains tax and how they apply on buy to let properties so that you can have the best chance. Some of these ways include using your tax-free allowance, seeing if you are eligible for private residence relief, jointly owning the buy to let property with your spouse, cutting costs, and, as mentioned earlier, setting up a limited company.

As mentioned earlier, capital gains tax is applicable to any profit earned over the sale of non-inventory items priced over £6,000, putting them under the heading of valuable assets. Aside from property, stocks, and bonds, it could also be artwork and jewelry. However, it will not be applicable to the profit earned over the sale of a motor car. Capital gains tax is also applicable on the sale of a residential property, but with the availability of private residence relief, most people do not pay CGT on the sale of their primary residential property. According to regulations, the payment of CGT on the sale of a buy to let property must be reported within 60 days as of October 27, 2021. Previously, this was 30 days. Ideally, you should not delay reporting the sale of the buy to let property before the tax year concludes. Within these 60 days, you need to report and pay the correct CGT to HM Revenue & Customs (HMRC), which is more than enough time to make the correct calculations. If you fail to follow the correct procedure and timeline, and do not comply with the regulations within the same tax year, you will be facing a penalty as well as paying additional interest.

To illustrate how this works, say you sell your buy to let in March 2020. That means you have until the deadline of filing your tax return for the tax year of 2020–21 to notify the HMRC of the sale and pay the capital gains tax. But according to the new rules, if the property was sold on October 28, 2021, the same process needs to be completed within 60 days, i.e. by December 21, 2021. Technically, it is an improvement over the previous regulations which only offered 30 days, but it is still a nine-month reduction.

Capital gains tax varies for basic-rate and higher-rate taxpayers, i.e. 18% and 28% respectively on the profit upon the sale of the property. The profit is any amount adding on to the value of the property since the present owner's purchase. The good news is that, if you ever sell your buy to let property, you can avail a capital gains allowance of £12,300. This is available to every taxpayer as of the tax year of 2022–23. You can also offset certain permitted costs such as the Stamp Duty of your original purchase, expenses paid for improvements to the property such as building an extension, making a new kitchen, improving energy efficiency, and more, and fees paid to estate agents and solicitors for selling the property. However, you won't be able to offset any expenses made for mortgage repayments and the maintenance of the property.

Capital gains tax is also applicable if you reinvest the profit you make from the sale of the buy to let property into another property. However, CGT won't apply to the total amount you receive from the sale. To clarify, deduct the amount you paid for the property when you first bought it, along with additional costs such as Stamp Duty, estate agent and solicitor's fees, and the remaining amount, i.e. the profit, will be subject to capital gains tax.

If you want to reduce the capital gains tax on selling your buy to let property, start by using your tax-free capital gains allowance of £12,300. Once you use it in the present tax year, you won't be able to carry it forward into the future tax years. If you have used the tax-free allowance partially or completely and are planning to sell the property, it is recommended to hold off on the sale. Moreover, you can double your tax-free capital gains allowance to £24,600 by owning the property jointly with your spouse.

You can also check if you are eligible for private residence relief (PRR). This is available to any landlord who turned their buy to let property into their principal residence prior to selling it, as it allows the landlord-turned-resident owner to claim relief for the years they lived in the property. In addition, the owner can also claim private residence relief for nine months before selling. To illustrate, let's say you acquired a buy to let property in March 2012 at £350,000. When you sell it in March 2022 at the price of £500,000, you earn a profit of £150,000. If you lived in said property for five years and rented it for the remaining five, you can claim PRR for the 60 months you lived there, and an additional nine months before selling. Therefore, you can claim PRR for a total of 69 months.

On the other hand, you can also qualify for lettings relief of up to £40,000 if you were living in the same property as your tenant. To use the same example as above, if you rented out the property for five years and also lived there in a separate unit, you then need to decide the portion of the property that was rented out. In this scenario, you need to decide what portion of your home you rented out, so you can decide that 20% of your property was rented to the tenant. This way, you can only claim PRR on 80% of your total profit of £75,000 of those five years, which comes to £60,000. However, you can also claim letting relief for the remaining £15,000. Do note that the HMRC can disallow PRR to anyone if they believe an applicant is claiming it only as a tax dodge.

Then, there is the Inheritance Tax, i.e. the tax on the assets of a deceased person, including property, possession, and money. Buy to let properties are also subject to inheritance tax (IHT) as they become part of your estate upon your death. IHT is charged at 40% if the total value of your assets is £325,000 and over, which can run up a substantial tax collection. Furthermore, if you decide on selling these properties to reduce the IHT, you end up paying capital gains tax on the sale instead. Not only that, you will have to pay IHT on the revenue you make from the sale of the property as it becomes part of your estate, assuming you don't spend it all before dying.

You could try gifting the properties or the money you made from their sale to your next of kin, but that would require that you live for a further seven years after the gifting. If you pass away within those seven years, the gift will not be exempt from inheritance tax and will fall upon the recipient of the gift, essentially passing the buck to your heirs. On the plus side, the inheritance tax will vary depending on the number of years you lived after gifting the property or the money. In the case of jointly owning a buy to let property, both owners would have to live for seven years after gifting the property or money, as the value is divided between the co-owners, i.e. you and your spouse. However, under no circumstances should you try selling the property for less than the market value to your next of kin.

Mortgaging the Buy to Let

In the second chapter, the details regarding how a buy to let mortgage differed from standard residential mortgages was reviewed. There are other important factors that you need to recognize if you are buying your very first buy to let. To begin with, mortgage companies are wary of providing first-time buyers with such a mortgage due to certain risks they have considered beforehand. This means that, though there should theoretically be no problem for first-time buyers to get a buy to let mortgage, it is incredibly difficult in reality for first-time buyers to let investors to qualify. Mortgage companies need a large deposit between 15% and 25% of the value of the property in order to consider a buy to let mortgage. This is a substantially high rate compared to the 5% of the property value for a standard residential mortgage.

Moreover, mortgage companies also verify whether or not first-time buyers are literally first-time buyers, i.e. they do not own any property whatsoever. Companies will then examine a buyer's circumstances thoroughly to determine why they haven't owned their own home until this point, and why they are interested in acquiring a buy to let property.

As reviewed in the previous chapter, mortgage companies also set the condition for the monthly rental income to be over 125% to 150% of the monthly mortgage payment. The exact percentage varies based on your tax rate, the kind of property you are mortgaging, and whether or not you are purchasing through a limited company. Mortgage companies require evidence that you can fulfill such a rental amount in the form of documentation such as bank statements showing inflows of rental income. This could be if you are purchasing an existing buy to let with tenants already present or if you are mortgaging a buy to let property later on.

Mortgage companies also prefer buyers who are making at least £25,000 each year. Interestingly, the minimum age requirement for applying for a buy to let mortgage is 18 years, however, some mortgage companies refuse applicants under 25 years of age or over 75 years of age. This is not a standard for every mortgage company; these preferences vary. They will also focus on the type of tenancies the buyer-turned-landlord will offer, particularly short-term, single assured tenancies. Not every mortgage company will work for you if you are planning to mortgage an HMO or a holiday let. You will need to seek out a specialist mortgage lender for this purpose.

If you feel that you meet the above criteria, you should start preparing the relevant paperwork for the mortgage application.

This includes proof of identification, proof of income such as salary slips or an SA302, latest bank statements, and details of any outstanding debts. You should also inquire from the mortgage company if they require any other documents. These are typically mentioned on their websites or in the literature provided by them, but make sure to confirm from the mortgage company representative you are dealing with.

It is also helpful if you can provide any credentials of your landlord experience; however, this does not guarantee that your application will be successful. Furthermore, experienced or professional landlords who have a portfolio of at least four mortgaged rental properties are referred to as portfolio landlords. These landlords have further documentation requirements, such as details of alternative sources of income as well as any personal source of income, evidence of tax payment on the rental income, and the relevant tax returns. Professional landlords also need to submit a detailed summary of the property portfolio including the value of the properties, the addresses of the properties, the received rent, and the mortgage amount of the properties, as well as the expenses involved in managing the properties. These include payments to estate agents, solicitors, accountants, insurance payments, maintenance charges, and so on. Aside from these, professional landlords should also be able to provide a cash flow projection, a statement of assets and liabilities, and a sound business plan.

In the past, any property being rented out with three or more floors and occupied by five or more people from a minimum of two households would require a license. With the changes in regulation, this license requirement does not take into consideration the size and space of the property. Instead, the license will be required for any property with five or more people belonging to two or more households.

At present, mortgage companies offer buy to let mortgages to an individual with one property who offers short-term single assured tenancies, as well as limited companies with buy to let properties. Both these mortgages are similar in many ways, however, in the limited company buy to let mortgage, the mortgage is borrowed through a limited company in order to reduce the tax charges. Nevertheless, it is important to discuss whether or not you should consider getting a mortgage through a limited company by speaking to your account or tax advisor. If you are a professional landlord with a portfolio of four or more rental properties, you are eligible for a portfolio buy to let mortgage. Aside from these, certain mortgage companies also offer financing for HMOs and holiday lets, but not all of them specialize in these.

Keep in mind that the mortgage fees for buy to let properties can be significantly higher than those of a standard mortgage. For one thing, these mortgages do not come under the Financial Conduct Authority (FCA), and for another, these mortgages are offered as interest-based only. If the interest rates increase, your mortgage company will want to know whether or not you can make the mortgage payments. For this, you should calculate the rental yield to show that your property, location, and target audience will earn you enough of a profit to be eligible for a buy to let mortgage under the conditions reviewed above.

To calculate the rental yield, start with the yearly rental income, then divide it for the property price you paid, and multiply it by 100 to get a percentage. This yield won't cover the additional costs such as maintenance, service charges, and mortgage interest, not to mention any time the property is vacant and you are not making any rent. Some people suggest cashing in their pension pot to finance a buy to let property instead of going to a mortgage company. But this also has certain challenges; if you withdraw your pension, you will have to pay income tax on 75% of it, while 25% is tax-free.

Again, always be ready to consult with a professional such as an estate agent or a mortgage broker to find out what the best solution is for your needs.

Chapter 6:

Buying New or Refurbishing

Buy to Let and The City

If you have lived all your life in London and have identified a potential tenant market in the capital, it's not that far-fetched that you would want to start your buy to let business there. Having said that, starting a buy to let business in the city is not a piece of cake. If you are not aware of all the risks, costs, and efforts involved in it, you will find yourself in a very serious and heartbreaking situation.

Let's get the first thing out of the way: London is not cheap. Not for residents, not for tenants, not for property owners, not for anyone. According to the Land Registry House Price Index, London has almost double the property price average than the rest of the UK, standing at £552,755 in August 2022 compared to the UK average of £295,903 in the same month. To put that into perspective, the average price in August 2022 in the South East was £406,981, £364,885 in the East of England, £335,927 in the South West, £255,202 in the West Midlands, £255,114 in the East Midlands, £219,025 in the North West, £212,313 in Yorks & Humber, and £164,395 in the North East. First-time buyers paid on average £476,248 in August 2022 against the average of £262,022 for England overall. According to Halifax, the average deposit paid by first-time buyers in London during 2021 was £115,759, more than double the average deposit paid in the UK of £53,935. Needless to say, these figures have not gone down.

The Land Registry also details the average prices within London in the different boroughs. The least expensive borough is Barking and Dagenham with an average property price of £354,052 in August 2022, whereas the most expensive in the same month was Kensington and Chelsea with an average property price of £1,336,232. In between these two extremes, property prices in Bexley averaged at £404,141, £420,869 in Newham, £426,861 in Croydon, £428,076 in Havering, £530,416 in Bromley, £585,394 in Merton, £669,429 in Hackney, £799,573 in Hammersmith and Fulham, £810,106 in the City of London, £867,771 in Camden, and £964,079 in Westminster.

That's only one part of the price of living in The City. There are all sorts of additional costs such as council tax, mortgage rates, commuting, and so on, that make London an intimidating prospect for first-time investors. The tax rates differ in each borough as the councils have their own rates, which is why one is never sure which one is cheaper till they go conduct their own research. The Ministry of Housing, Communities & Local Government website has an extensive list of rates of council tax bands which should help you understand what would suit your goals better.

Apart from taxes, mortgage companies tend to refuse any applications for certain properties in London, or at least make it very difficult for anyone to get a mortgage for such properties. These include new-build properties, studio flats, and short leases. With new-build properties, mortgage companies impose stricter limits on how much you can borrow from them, which can be as low as 85% value of a house or 75% of a flat. Compared to this, older properties can get mortgaged as high as 95% of the property value. An obvious reason is that new-build properties lose some value in the early years of ownership, therefore mortgage companies prefer not to take on such a risk. Another no-brainer is any property that is in a state of disrepair and unlivable. The most basic requirement of a livable dwelling is a fully-functioning kitchen, bathroom, and a sturdy and leak-proof roof. Needless to say, mortgage companies will not be willing to finance any such properties.

London also sees an increasing demand for studio flats as they provide a kind of minimalism for a niche clientele. This includes people who prefer living in a compact-sized apartment and have a limited budget, plus it is not that expensive to furnish one, making them ideal for single working professionals living in The City. However, once such residents decide that they want to have a change in their lives, like getting married or relocating, the only other person who can buy a studio flat from them is someone in similar circumstances. Due to this, studio flats don't find a ton of buyers ready to pick it up and therefore mortgage companies hesitate to finance one. Apart from outright rejecting a mortgage application for studio flats, mortgage companies can add extra criteria which aren't that easy to meet, such as minimum floor space, particularly if the property is less than 30 square meters in size.

New builds sometimes face resistance even if they promote an off-the-grid living solution. Any property using generators as a power source is not easy to sell, while most people have not gotten on board with the idea of being cut off from the power grid. That said, newer builds themselves are great investments considering the kind of amenities they provide, as well as the assurance that they meet up-to-date construction and safety standards. This makes newer builds more sought after by potential tenants.

Then, there are properties with short leases, i.e. any lease under 80 years. You might be thinking that 80 years is a substantial amount of time, but it isn't the same when it comes to leases. If the lease drops below 80 years—also known as the "80-year-rule"—then the cost involved in extending it increases. Extending a short lease is very much possible, but the process itself is complex and requires expert attention, not to mention cost. This makes selling a property with a short lease challenging to sell, ergo a concern for mortgage companies to finance. If you are a landlord who only plans to benefit from the buy to let rental income for the next few decades, you don't need to extend the lease. That said, the value of the property drops if the lease drops under the 80-year threshold.

There are other properties in The City that can be difficult to mortgage, no matter how appealing they are to buyers financially. Ex-local authority housing, for instance, are less expensive compared to other homes, however, these properties tend to lose their value with the passage of time; hence the reason why they become appealing to buyers. Sellers, on the other hand, will find that they may not even earn a profit on an ex-local authority housing property, and at worst they stand to lose on their investment. Aside from that, ex-local housing properties are usually surrounded by other rented council houses, which makes them unappealing for mortgage companies to finance. Instead, they much prefer properties that are occupied by owners.

Another obvious choice are high-rise flats that come with their own set of pros and cons, not including the mortgage-related ones. Mortgage companies reserve the right to refuse any financing if a property or flat is above a certain floor or level in the building; with some companies refusing any flats between the fourth and the 20th floor. This varies among the mortgage companies, but the fact remains that high-rise flats have a sort of reputation with mortgage lenders particularly related to their resale value. High-rise flats are not just considered very vulnerable in an economic downturn, but also highly risky with the kind of neighborhood they are located in. Property owners have very little control over the high-rise building's owner and tenant make-up, which can create a volatile situation for investors, as the people living there have their own sets of problems, further exacerbated if said building is one of several other high-rises in the same area.

Another reason why high-rise properties don't qualify for mortgages is that they were constructed with material that is not up to the current standard. In the '60s and '70s, which is when most high-rises were built, concrete was used as the principal material. The same goes for any properties with steel or wood frames or thatched properties, as they do not meet the modern standards. It's a shame, as there are some iconic high-rise monuments that most people feel a great affinity for, including the Barbican Complex. Built over a 35-acre area in the heart of London that had been bombed by Nazi Germany during WWII, the Barbican Complex has around 2,000 flats that can fetch a lucrative sum; and is peppered with schools, theaters, art galleries, and more. Nevertheless, mortgage companies are reluctant to finance any units there.

The attitudes of mortgage companies also appear similar to any residential properties that are located above a commercial enterprise, such as restaurants, greengrocers, shops, cafes, bakeries, and pubs. This has been a recurring theme following the financial crisis, however, mortgage companies usually cite other issues like the smell, rubbish, noise, fumes, and other environmental concerns that are commonly associated with eateries. Moreover, the above businesses see a lot of daily foot traffic, which makes these properties a security concern, no matter how many assurances the prospective buyer or property owner can provide.

Pros and Cons of HMOs

Setting up your buy to let property as a house of multiple occupation (HMO) is also a great way to maximize your rental income. The way it works is that you can let out different rooms to individual households or to multiple house sharers in a single property and you can charge a higher rent from each of them. They will have access to communal areas such as lounge, kitchen, and bathrooms, as well as the entrance lobby if there is one. On the other hand, buy to lets are normally rented out as a whole to a single couple, family, or a small number of individual sharers—usually not more than three.

This is how you can get a three times higher yield out of an HMO through multiple rents from many individual tenants or more tenants sharing a single property. Neighborhoods close to universities that see a consistent intake of students from other towns are a thriving hotbed for HMOs, making them a practical and attractive alternative to traditional buy to lets. BVA BDRC, a London-based international business and consumer insight consultancy, suggests that the average rental yield of an HMO is 7.5%, compared to 3.6 for buy to lets as a whole during 2020 and 2021. Rental yield is the potential rental income that a landlord can expect out of a buy to let and will be discussed in detail in the following chapter.

With an HMO, you also don't have to worry about longer periods where one unit is vacant. Unlike a standard buy to let, HMOs are rented out on a single-room basis. Therefore, you could still make a great rental yield out of your remaining tenants—usually in the majority—that will cover all your overheads, though it may affect your profit margins slightly. Also, if you have researched your target market and location right, you can expect another tenant to start staying once you have the property listed as available to let. Your existing tenants could also refer someone looking for a place to live, thereby giving you a steady intake of potential tenants.

If you rent your HMO using a joint AST, voids are also likely to be lower as landlords can rely on more stable, reliable demand in the market for HMO properties. For example, if you rent to students, you can be fairly certain of strong and consistent demand at predictable intervals, as well as guaranteed minimum tenancy terms with your tenants who will need the property for at least the length of the academic year.

A good idea is to find an HMO that is up for sale with tenants already in place. This way, you are taking over from an existing, well-running business with tenants who are signed on to stay for a tenure and pay their rents responsibly. Once you become the landlord, you can carry on their existing tenancy agreements till the terms expire, following which you can have them sign a brand new tenancy agreement with terms and rent suitable to you. Furthermore, you will essentially take over all the responsibilities from the previous landlord such as managing the tenants, handling the maintenance, scheduling inspection work, and more.

On the other hand, you could also buy a single-family home and, once you fulfill the required license requirements and carry out the necessary safety regulation inspections and certifications, convert it into an HMO. From there, you can rent out individual rooms within the property to different tenants after all the above-mentioned requirements are fulfilled. Much like other buy to lets, the pricing for HMOs depends on the size of the property, the location, the amount of renovation or refurbishment it requires, the proximity to transport networks and other essential services, as well as Stamp Duty, fees, furnishings, compliance certifications and assessments, and the most important of all for HMOs, an HMO license.

When converting a single-family house to an HMO, you have to make it livable for a group of people sharing single communal spaces while also retaining their privacy in their rooms. This includes having fully-functioning bathrooms and kitchen that can accommodate the needs of all the tenants, upgrading or repairing your existing electrical and gas systems, making proper provisions for fire safety and emergency exits, and, if you are offering a fully furnished HMO, provide brand new and sturdy furniture, fixtures, and fittings.

Keep in mind that, with the number of tenants in your HMO, there will be far more wear and tear to your property's installations considering that not every tenant is going to be as responsible as the next. With one family living in a standard buy to let property, they would need to use the kitchen appliances, such as the stove, once or twice a day. But in an HMO, each independent tenant would use it whenever they find it convenient, possibly one after the other or for longer durations at a time. For instance, if five individual tenants use the stove whenever they need to, the increased use would add more wear and tear to the stove, making it necessary to get a new one fairly soon. The same goes for other appliances, such as the microwave, refrigerator, boiler, and more. On the plus side, it is possible to claim these maintenance expenses in your tax return.

This goes to show that, while you get a higher rental yield with an HMO, maintaining one is going to cost you more than a standard buy to let. Compared to a standard buy to let, you cannot rent out an HMO that isn't fully furnished, as the tenants will need everything sorted for them. With families, you can expect them to make the place feel like home, which is why they will add more of their furnishings to it. But with multiple individual tenants such as students who won't be staying there for a longer term and on a budget, they won't bring along much.

Aside from maintenance and other concerns, your time as an HMO landlord requires more time with paperwork and administration. This includes creating new rental contracts, handling deposits, taking stock of rent checks, and more. As HMOs have a higher turnover with students leaving term after term, this work increases as you have to maintain ledgers for completely new students after their short-term tenancies wind up. Therefore, be prepared to put in a lot more time and energy in looking after the management of your HMO, as it could turn into a full-time job for you once you realize how well the rental yields work out for you.

That said, it doesn't come without its risks. With multiple people living in a single property, you have to factor in how well they get along with each other, how responsibly they take care of the appliances and furnishings, and how likely they might be to breach the terms of the tenancy agreement. Students can be a particularly unpredictable bunch, especially if they start using prohibited substances. Even smoking in the premises irresponsibly can constitute a fire safety hazard. Any accidents or incidents within the property would come back to you and there is every chance that your license might get suspended if something critical happens, such as a fire or an explosion.

Renovating and Refurbishing a Buy to Let

Considering all the above kinds of properties that will be a challenge to fetch a mortgage for, your next best bet is to renovate or refurbish a buy to let property. Keep in mind that you won't be able to get a normal buy to let mortgage if the property you are looking to buy requires major renovations or refurbishments to make it livable. Any property that requires slight renovation should benefit you in terms of price. You can negotiate a lower price for such a property and save more than enough to carry out the necessary renovation work. Existing landlords can also refurbish their rental property to boost value, make it more attractive for tenants, and ask for a higher rental.

However, it is necessary to understand that there are similarities and differences between renovations and refurbishments. Depending on the kind of work that is taking place, both terms could cover all kinds of work to a property such as changing decorations, adding new carpeting, repairing doors and windows, changing kitchen and bathroom fixtures, knocking down walls, or adding extensions. But while renovations usually involve restoring and repairing any existing fixtures or furnishings so that they can return to a good condition, refurbishments create an opportunity for property owners to make changes and improvements to the existing fixtures and layout of a property through heavier repairs and replacements.

This brings up the concept of light and heavy refurbishments. As the names suggest, decorative work that doesn't interfere with the existing structure and layout of a property is referred to as light refurbishment. You do not need any kind of planning permission, and light refurbishments do not violate any building regulations. Examples of light refurbishments include replacing carpets or other floor coverings, upgrading kitchens and bathrooms, and repainting the walls or applying wallpaper. Furthermore, you can also apply for bridging finance for light refurbishments, provided that you are able to have the work completed at the earliest.

On the other hand, heavy refurbishments will require making major structural changes to the property. This includes building an extension, making changes to the supporting walls, knocking walls down, and rebuilding the roof, which would also require planning permission. To be considered a heavy refurbishment, the cost has to be over 15% of the property value. Though bridging finance is available for a standard maximum of 12 months, lenders can also offer up to 18 to even 36 months, which will give you enough time to obtain the planning permission.

As the existing owner of a buy to let with a buy to let mortgage, you can remortgage the property to get enough financing for the refurbishment work. This means extending the mortgage tenure and paying it off till the new date while you get the necessary finance to make improvements to the property. Keep in mind that if your mortgage is still far away from completing its term, there will be additional costs to remortgaging. Also, this usually works if your agreed-upon mortgage is not that large, and the extension to the mortgage will take into account the current value of the property and the rental income.

However, if you are buying a property that needs renovation or refurbishment, you won't be able to get a standard buy to let mortgage before the work is finished. There are other options available, such as a refurb-to-let loan. This is also referred to as a bridge-to-let or a short-term-to-let loan. You will first get a short-term bridging loan to help you finance the refurbishment to the property, after which the loan switches over to a standard buy-to-let mortgage. The refurb-to-let helps you make upgrades to a property or make a run-down, unlivable property into a perfect, livable condition. These upgrades can include physical changes, addition to amenities and utilities, improvements to energy saving, adherence to energy efficiency standards and safety standards, and more.

Though an attractive proposition, refurb-to-let loans have their limits. They are not granted if there is a need for planning permission or building regulations approval. Furthermore, refurb-to-let loans are a niche offering and there aren't many financing companies that provide them, making it very difficult to get suitable terms. Refurb-to-let loans also don't work if the cost of refurbishment is over 25% of the property value. Other refurbishment bridging loans provide up to 70% of the Gross Development Value. (GDV). This value signifies how much the property will be worth after refurbishment and renovations. They can be processed in under a week, which makes them ideal if you need to secure faster finance.

Do remember that lenders providing refurbishment bridging loans also take other factors into consideration, such as whether or not you already own the property, how much refurbishment work is required, and whether or not you plan to apply for a buy to let mortgage once the work is done.

The Pros of New Builds

If refurbishing or renovating an older property seems like such a hassle, then investing in a new build offers several advantages and value. New builds have been gaining greater ground across the UK, with around 50,000 new homes built in early 2021.

Developers are constantly coming up with new projects that make buying properties a lot easier.

One of the benefits of new builds is that developers encourage buyers with extra incentives that include free carpeting, paying Stamp Duty, installing new LED lights, and more. An added benefit to the purchasing process is that the prospective buyer will be the first owner, so they won't have to worry about who the previous buyers were and what condition they kept the property in. You also stand to gain more capital growth if you plan to buy a new build three years prior, i.e. in the first phase, to the build's completion in a regeneration area.

Another benefit of new builds is that buyers can mold them to their ideal vision. For landlords, a new build provides a great opportunity to set the property up for their target market. All you get with most new builds are a ready-built house with new tiling and paintwork, plus a fully functioning kitchen and bathrooms. From there, landlords can add the necessary furnishings they need to attract their desired tenants without having to get into the hassle of light or heavy refurbishments.

The keyword with new builds is "new," ergo you can rest assured the property is up-to-date, offers most modern conveniences, and delivers great value in the long-term. New builds are constructed using the latest components such as construction material, plumbing, gas piping, and electrical wiring, and all of them have to comply with present-day safety and energy efficiency regulations. At present, 80% of new builds have the highest A or B Energy Performance Certificate (EPC) ratings (HomeOwners Alliance, n.d.). This also allows tenants to save on energy bills while builders can equip new builds with modern smart home technology that adds more panache to the house.

All new builds also have warranties that cover the first two years for the defects insurance period, while a 10-year structural insurance period kicks off from the date of completing the purchase. The defects insurance period helps landlords in case there are issues with improperly sealed windows, faulty heating pipes, and more, making it the builder's responsibility to repair them. Once the defects insurance period elapses after two years, the structural insurance period comes into effect, where only major problems will be the builder's responsibility, including the foundations, load-bearing parts of the floors, ceilings, roofs, the external renders, and chimneys. Any other non-structural defects such as problems with fixtures, fittings, or drainage will be the landlord's responsibility.

Work Checklist and Cost

Every renovation and refurbishment project is going to be different, but most of them go through the same stages. Once you find a property you are interested in, you will need an architect or contractor to get their evaluation about what kind of work would increase the longevity and marketability of the property. This requires thorough attention-to-detail and looking at every inch of the property for any flaws or threats such as molds, rot, infestations, issues with structural integrity, seepage, and more. Contractors and architects can identify these issues before you make your plans and ask for permission so that you know exactly how much work is required, what kind of permissions you will need, and what your budget will end up being. Based on their expert recommendations, you can then approach the local planning department with regards to planning permission for any heavy refurbishment.

Finding a property that requires one thing, but it is also important to evaluate the location of the property. If you are looking at a run-down property in a high-end neighborhood or street, modernizing the property will increase the resale value based on the refurbishment work as well as the reputation of the neighborhood. Furthermore, you should also inquire from the planning department whether or not your planned refurbishment work will be allowed or not. If you invest into such a property but the planning permission is rejected, your entire plans can go up in smoke. You can consult with a planning expert to find out if the relevant planning department usually provides permission for the kind of work you are planning to do and then confirm with the local authority before you make a decision.

Once you acquire the needed financing and receive the planning permissions, you can then start work. Your contractor and architect should draw up comprehensive plans but they will essentially involve taking everything apart as much as possible and keeping everything that is in good condition. Structural changes could involve knocking down walls for an open-plan layout, adding an extension to the property, converting it into a lot, and adding more support beams and walls if you can to create more private space.

As the structure and layout is being improved, you can then stand by with the work for upgrading the electrical and heating systems. This will involve making improvements in the gas supply, making sure that the heating system is safe and up to standard, ensuring electrical wiring safety across the property, and meeting the energy efficiency standards as discussed in Chapter 4. At the same time, you should make sure that the water and drainage systems are also updated and working properly. Leaky pipes, dripping taps, and smells from the drains should be looked into, as well as any signs of mold or asbestos in the kitchen and bathrooms.

Once the structural work and concealed piping and wiring networks are nearing completion, you can then get to the fixtures, flooring, and paint. The flooring will be next, which will involve checking any squeaky floors and stairs, fixing up loose tiles, or installing new tiles completely. If your property needs drywall and plastering, then that will be next before you can either paint the walls or apply wallpaper. The same goes for any peeling paint and cracks to the walls and ceiling. Following the paintwork, your next priority will be fixing up any doors and windows that are squeaking or sticking, updating the latches and locks, and replacing broken or damaged windows. Installing new fixtures in the kitchen and bathroom should happen once all the paint work is done.

Most of the external work will also be cosmetic, such as paint and plastering, however, make sure that there are no compromises to the external structure such as cracks, mold, leaks, and more.

The major considerations to make are related to cost. Renovating and refurbishing a property can run up a bill of tens of thousands of pounds, depending on how much work is required. More expenses include paying the architect for their services and creating a design, paying contractors for their time and work, paying the relevant permission fees to the planning department, among others. The quality of work and the people you hire will also make a huge difference to the overall GDV, however, the investment to ensure this will also be on the higher side.

Renovating or refurbishing a run-down property offers a great deal of satisfaction, as you can create something with the potential to be worth more than it already is. It allows you to add a great deal of value to the property itself, as well as the neighborhood, as more and more people become attracted to it. The benefit of buying a run-down property is that you can remodel it to how you would like it to be for your potential tenants and what it can offer them in terms of comfort and value. Your property has to become something worth paying a profitable rental for. Each pound you spend on property can impact its resale value. A new kitchen worth £10,000 has the potential to add £20,000 to £30,000 to the property's asking price, while a loft extension worth £30,000 or a or a new bathroom can give you an advantage of £100,000 on the asking price.

That said, even the best laid plans often find hiccups and surprises along the way. The work itself is tiring and frustrating, given the fact that you could end up overspending on your estimated budget. You should factor in a 20% cushion over your budget just in case there are any unforeseen expenses or issues. Usually, buyers feel confident that every point has been examined thoroughly, but every now and then a problem arises, mostly when the work gets underway. Perhaps the extent of the structural work was much more than originally anticipated, or the electrical system will need a complete rewiring instead of repairs. A lot of things are not discovered till the place is taken apart. Moreover, as a landlord, you will want to be as involved as possible, as you are not only spending your money on the refurbishment, but you also want the final result to be perfect so that you can envision your buy to let business become successful. But the more personally involved you get, the more grueling and frustrating the whole work will feel to you. You will be in the thick of it; where all the work is taking place and want everything as you envision it, running the risk of micromanaging the operation instead of trusting the experts working there. If you have never experienced work being done on a property before, you may find yourself out of your depth and also discover that there is a different approach to dealing with contractors and workmen.

Therefore, be sure to stock up on a lot of patience and trust in the people who are working for you while also being present to show them that you expect the best results, i.e. your money's worth.

Chapter 7:

Working Out the Financials

Return on Investment

After having your buy to let property ready for business, i.e. by putting in the money, time, and effort to make it as attractive to and livable for tenants as possible, renting it out is the next step. Your property needs to start making money as soon as it is ready to be habited, as mortgage repayments depend on the cash inflows from a rental income. Nevertheless, a rental income—or rental yield—is only one of two ways in which you make money. Your rental yield is the percentage of money you receive in rent.

You can calculate your rental yield by taking the rental income per year and dividing it by the property purchase price. The result will be converted to a percentage after you multiply it by 100. To illustrate, take a property worth £400,000 after all the renovations and refurbishment. If the annual rental income is £40,000, you will have to deduct your overheads so that you can find out how much you take away with you. Taking £20,000 as your overhead, you will still be making £20,000, which makes a rental yield of 5%.

At present, the average rental yield in the UK is 3.63%, which differs from place to place. Anything higher than the average is considered a high-yield rental area. Whatever the rental yield is, you have to take into account your outgoing expenses including mortgage repayments, insurance, maintenance, fees for estate and letting agents and accountants, and more.

When doing your research for potential properties, your projected rental yield is going to play a huge part in your decision to invest in a particular buy to let. Naturally, your first thought is going to be trying to find a property in a high-yield area, however, that can be a lot more challenging. You will find that the property prices themselves are on the higher side and mortgage companies will have their own terms when they evaluate you as a potential landlord. Other factors such as the location of the buy to let, how often you can expect periods of property vacancy and how long or short they are, what contractors you use to carry out services, maintenance, and renovation, what your credit rating is like, and more, also affect your total rental yield. Still, you can investigate parts of the country with greater rental yields by inquiring from an estate agent or checking property websites. Start with looking into your own town or city first to see what kind of rental yield you can expect. If you find one that also checks the boxes for the kind of property you want and the tenants you aim to serve, make an offer.

The second way you can make a return on your investment is capital growth. This is the amount of money your property stands to make once you decide to sell it in the future. Capital growth is governed through various factors such as rising prices due to inflation, market trends, demand and supply of affordable accommodation, and the overall value of your buy to let property as a business venture. The most immediate buyer for your property will be another landlord who is looking to either start in the business or expand their holdings. The main consideration such a buyer will make is whether or not your property has a significant rental yield as they will want to make the most money out of it. This is why your buy to let needs to be making a lot of money consistently so that it can become attractive to potential investors. With a successfully running business, you can expect several bids to your property once you decide to sell up.

Don't forget that any property you sell that isn't your home will be subject to Capital Gains tax, not to mention the tax on your rental income. That should also be a consideration when working out your rental yield as you need to keep abreast of the changing tax regulations and your circumstances. Keep a close eye on tax laws or ask your accountant to advise you regarding how any prevailing tax regulations will affect the sale of your buy to let property.

There is also a possibility that you will want to cash out much earlier than you had planned for, thus making you access the funds already invested in your buy to lets. It could be due to an emergency or a major health concern within the family that could put you in the position where you will need a large amount of cash. Unfortunately, it will not be that straightforward. If you sell your property with tenants living there, you can only sell to other landlords looking to get into the buy to let business. You could try vacating the property before selling, but there is a strict process in place. Also, following the COVID-19 pandemic, new rules have been put in place where tenants cannot be vacated in the initial tenancy period. Furthermore, you will also have to give your tenants six months notice before vacating the property. The only other option you could have is to extend your mortgage period, however, mortgage companies reserve the right to decline any such requests.

The Demand for Buy to Lets

Based on data from London-based luxury estate agency Hamptons, the year 2022 has seen a resurgence in property demand following the unforeseen turn it took during the COVID-19 pandemic. Compared to the pre-pandemic period of 2019, Britain has seen an investment worth £8.5 billion in property in the first three months of 2022. That's roughly around 43,000 homes across the country and twice as high as 2019. More data suggests that this is the first time people have bought more property than sold since 2016.

Following the pandemic, people have been seeing a return to The City en masse, which has created a frenzy in looking for affordable buy to let accommodation, particularly flats. The waiting periods for viewings have also been on the rise, as estate agents are trying to facilitate as many potential tenants as possible. This is as a result of a decline in the rental market due to frequent changes in taxation and regulations, prompting buy to let investors to pack up and sell out their assets over the years. In 2017, rental properties soared to an all-time high of 5.3 million. These have been shrinking down over time to a present day 300,000, which has created a shortage of buy to lets amidst a throng of desiring tenants. In March 2022, there was a shortage of buy to lets by 44%, compared to the same time last year, while there was a decline of over 50% in hotspots such as Camden, Hackney, Islington, and Lambeth.

Not only has this created a shortage of buy to lets to fill in the demand-to-supply gap, it has also shot up the rental prices of the available buy to let spaces. Even though this increase is expected to simmer down as people also have to consider their cost of living, it doesn't change the fact that tenant demand is not being met. Rentals of a new buy to let in Britain peaked at

£1,115 per month in March 2022 compared to £1,022 same time last year. There has also been a surge in Inner London rents as they reached an average of £2,571 per month; a 21.3% growth. North East showed the highest gross rental yield of 9%, while the rest of England saw a rental yield of 6% overall. Landlords are certainly taking advantage of this and trying to grow their portfolios. This is an ideal time for you to find yourself a great buy to let to meet tenant demand.

That said, there is also stiff competition in the form of mortgage-based homeowners. The decline in buy to let properties have seen a converse growth in renters finally being able to buy their own homes for the first time. Since there has been a lack of affordable social housing for people with low incomes, buy to let properties have traditionally soared and garnered very high rents. But that has changed with affordable mortgage opportunities for first-time homeowners.

Tougher Restrictions on Financing

In Chapter 5, we reviewed that buy to let mortgages require a deposit between 15% and 25% of the value of the property, compared to the 5% of the property value for a standard residential mortgage. The bigger your initial deposit, the better mortgage rate you are likely to get. Anyone willing to invest a deposit of 40% of the property price can get incredible buy to let mortgage deals. There are rarely any buy to let mortgages out there that aren't provided on an interest-only basis, which means that you are required to pay the interest on the mortgage minus the capital every month. This benefits property owners, as you can reduce your monthly outflows. However, you will still need to pay off the loan when the mortgage term ends, or refinance the property instead.

If you are setting up a limited company to acquire buy to let properties, you can benefit from the tax cuts as well as wear-and-tear allowance. While there is only a small percentage of company-owned buy to let mortgages, the increase in their number shows that this is a far more viable option than owning buy to lets individually. But, as we have seen in earlier chapters, not everyone can decide one day to start a limited company for this purpose unless they are ready to build a large portfolio. For one thing, interest rates for limited companies can be much higher than those offered to individuals owning buy to lets.

If you cannot afford a 40% deposit, you will have to compare the various buy to let mortgage deals out there till you find one that has friendly terms for you. One important thing to remember is to calculate exactly how much the loan is going to cost you. While you may be attracted by a cheap initial interest rate, this is usually outset by very high upfront processing fees reaching as high as £1,999. Whereas some mortgage companies charge fixed high fees, others can charge a percentage of the amount borrowed instead—around 0.5%.

Despite attractive mortgage offers for buy to lets, one of the reasons why landlords had been selling off their assets prior to 2022 has been the strictness in affordability tests. This is largely due to stringent lending rules imposed by the Bank of England to bring the rising tide of buy to let investments to a halt, thus creating harsher restrictions for new entrants in the market. Mortgage companies now use Interest Cover Ratios (ICRs) to calculate the profitability and viability of a landlord's buy to let property. This ICR covers the landlord's mortgage payments out of their rental income. It is tested at a representative interest rate, the most common being 5.5%. This is why the projected rental income is set at 125% of the mortgage payment by the lenders. But this doesn't stop many mortgage companies from setting a projected rental income as high as 145%.

The Bank of England has also classified professional landlords with a portfolio of four or more properties as such to make it difficult for them to get more financing. The rules for stress-testing portfolio landlords have also become more trying. Portfolio landlords must now present mortgage companies with projected cash flow information and business models for each individual property in their portfolio to apply for an extended mortgage or remortgage a property. This is a major change from before, where all portfolio landlords had to do was present their overall profit and loss numbers, making things much more difficult for professional landlords who have heavily mortgaged their properties.

Aside from the Bank of England restrictions, mortgage companies themselves vary their terms for portfolio landlords. Some mortgage companies, for instance, have put up a cap on the total number of properties a landlord can have in their portfolio. Usually, this limit is set to 10 properties. Other mortgage companies use different representative interest rates when calculating ICR based on how many properties there are in the portfolio, while some stipulate that the ICR needs to be over 100% for each property in the portfolio. Moreover, the rapid changes to tax regulations have made landlords think twice before adding more properties to their business. Instead, they have found it much more viable to remortgage their existing properties. This is largely due to the cuts in mortgage interest tax relief and the Stamp Duty surcharge of 3% on a second property.

The strictness in regulation has also been felt by many mortgage companies as they aim to attract more landlords towards buy to let mortgages. Some offer cuts on their upfront fees while others offer cashback options. Banks lending for buy to lets use a top-slicing system, whereby they consider a landlord's personal income in their affordability assessments. This personal income includes any salary or pension scheme which, if substantial, could be used to fill up any shortfall in affordability assessments. A mortgage broker will be able to advise you if this could help you get a better mortgage deal, as there aren't many financial institutions that offer top-slicing.

Interestingly, one can also become a landlord purely by circumstances without having foreseen it. The most common situation is when homeowners have had to rent out their residential homes due to difficult times, thus prompting them to apply for a buy to let mortgage or, if their house already has a standard mortgage, switch it to a buy to let one. In some cases, a person can also become a landlord by inheriting a buy to let property. Either way, you cannot continue an existing mortgage and will need to tell the mortgage company that the property has an outstanding owner-occupier mortgage. Failing to do so could result in your mortgage being invalidated. There is also a possibility that some mortgage companies could permit you to continue on your existing mortgage with a consent to let, thus allowing you to use your property as a buy to let without the relevant mortgage. This is something that varies based on individual circumstances, therefore it is vital you bring this up with your mortgage broker.

Chapter 8:

Building Your Buy to Let Portfolio

When it comes to building a business in buy to lets, or any property for that matter, you should be thinking of the long game. Why stick with one or two properties when you can have a larger business over a greater area that you can eventually sell for an incredible profit much later, or simply build an empire that can carry forward to creating generation wealth?

This is where making a property portfolio is the next logical step. Simply put, this is where you have a group of rental properties under your ownership, or that of a company that you own. Building a property investment portfolio provides a great return on investment not just by renting out the property to the tenants and making rental income, but also through the rise in property value of your rental asset over the course of time.

As said above, however, it is a long game. Building a property investment portfolio takes a lot of time, especially if you are a first-time investor, and also depends on what kind of decisions you make with your property, such as who your target tenant market is, what kind of buy to let you are acquiring and managing, how you are going to mortgage your properties, and how much you have budgeted for costs and service charges. Every investment decision you make plays a key role in the overall success of your buy to let business, which can ultimately chart out the path to creating a diverse property portfolio.

First, you have to evaluate where you are starting from. You could be a first-time entrant to the property business in general and the buy to let business in particular. If that is the case, then it is only natural for you to think big and dive in headfirst to what obviously seems like a lofty goal. However, at this early stage in the game, you should hold back before expanding too much too quickly. Focus on a growth plan and strategy that allows you to start small so that you are able to test the waters and gain more experience. This way, you learn both from successes and failures, and understand how to approach your next buy to let property after the first one. You also learn what steps not to take and also get advice on potential markets that you could set yourself up in.

On the other hand, you could already have a great deal of experience in the property business, which is when thinking of a buy to let portfolio is a sound plan. Granted, you will get to this point eventually after you start off in the buy to let industry, but it takes time, experience, and more confidence to take the necessary steps. Ultimately, buy to let portfolios are a long-term investment plan. Once you have the relevant experience and have gained enough confidence in yourself as a landlord and property service provider, you can then make decisions to expand into nearby or further territories by acquiring sound properties that you know will make great investments.

Once you start investing in potential properties further afield, you can see your property portfolio building up and set goals for the kind of revenue you foresee through the rental income.

It shouldn't take more than a couple of years for that revenue to materialize, making you a substantial amount of wealth and creating a profitable cash flow that you can leverage for further growth. Not only do you benefit from a reliable and continuous income in the form of rental payments, your property also accrues value over time, considering how much capital growth the property market offers. This will provide you a significant profit on your property if you ever plan to sell it.

You will also be able to take advantage of a booming economy that almost always leads to inflation, where your revised rental agreements with tenants can see a rise in rental income, giving you more returns. This inflation hedging may seem like overburdening your tenants, but it does make sound business sense as you have to keep your costs and profit margins in mind. However, that does not mean that you raise rents in a way that is considered unfair and unpayable by your existing tenants. Remember that the success of your business also depends upon the satisfaction level of your clients, i.e. your tenants, and how much you empathize with them. Find a healthy balance in raising rents that don't put either of you out of pocket too much.

One of the biggest advantages with a buy to let property portfolio is the ability to leverage your equity. This means that you can use the value of your existing rental properties and gather financing to buy more property, thus helping you grow your business and make more money. It will also give you an opportunity to diversify into various kinds of buy to lets that you had not done before when you were identifying your target market. For instance, if you had targeted single working professionals when you were starting out with your first buy to let, you can later consider investing in student lets somewhere else or holiday lets in the city. This will require that you do your research and find properties that are going to offer you the returns you expect, whether they are completely new prospects or if you are buying them from another landlord. With a diverse property portfolio, you minimize the risks of the changes in the rental market where one type of buy to let suffers a setback while another grows.

Buy to Let Portfolio Checklist

First and foremost, you are going to need a sizable investment capital if you are planning to build a buy to let property portfolio. Being financially ready is a no-brainer as, no matter what kind of property you plan to get into, you won't get anything for nothing. That said, you do not have to be wealthy in order to build this business. The goal here is to build your wealth by starting small and growing it over time. This is where utilizing the equity against your existing rental properties proves to be invaluable as you climb up the property ladder.

Even when you are starting out with your first buy to let, you have the option to leverage the equity in your own residential home so that you can pay the mortgage deposit for a buy to let. Most mortgage companies and banks provide a variety of mortgage options on friendly terms once they see that your buy to let business goals will see steady income and growth as the years go by, which makes mortgaging a buy to let the best option to get started. You can use the rental income to repay your mortgage and other costs, as well as turn over a profit for yourself that you can use to grow your business.

You should also set goals and Key Performance Indicators (KPIs) for what you expect out of your business. Your goals will vary from other landlords and portfolio investors in that you are either looking for consistent and substantial rental income or for expanding your capital and holdings. Once you have the particular goal set in mind, you can then chart out the steps necessary to reach there.

One important KPI in your buy to let business has to be the value of your income versus the expenses you are spending on. This is known as Positive Cash flow, meaning that your rental income should cover all your expenses and also earn you a profit. Under no circumstances should your outflows, i.e. your mortgage payment, maintenance cost, service fees, tax, and so on, be over your rental income. Granted, there can be unexpected maintenance costs, however, you have to be able to foresee any such issues by making sure that your property has undergone the necessary renovation and refurbishment, and also has the required quality standards and safety certifications.

Another unexpected situation which can cause a drop in Positive Cash Flow is when your property or unit is vacant due to no tenants for whatever reason. It could be because the tenants have moved on and you have not been able to find a new one immediately, or if the market has pushed rental payments out of reach for the average tenants. This is where diversification of your buy to let properties proves to be a boon, but it can only be assured if your investment decisions have not backfired. Then, there is the necessary calculation for Stamp Duty, Capital Gains Tax, and other payments. These need to be carefully budgeted with the help of a qualified accountant, otherwise it can put your entire business enterprise in danger. The most critical of this is if your mortgage companies decide to foreclose on your leveraged property, i.e. your residential house if you have mortgaged it, if you fail to meet your commitments and capitalize on your business.

Therefore, keep a vigil eye on your Positive Cash Flow and make sure you are checking off all your KPIs. Whether it is calculating the increase in rental incomes if you raise the rent or how much profit you can expect from selling a property, you need to stay on top of all the expenses that can be incurred out of your Positive Cash Flow and ensure that it is not going in the red zone, or negative.

The quality of your research before investing into a particular property is also going to make or break your business plans. You have to effectively gauge the potential returns of a buy to let property, as these will be the key to any future plans for investing in other properties. How savvy and confident you become in the buy to let arena, and where you get your advice from, will make future investments a lot easier and more considered. Keep your finger on the pulse of the buy to let market and take in as much information and updates about the changing winds as much as possible. Your existing network of professionals such as estate agents, accountants, and legal representatives should be able to advise you of any major changes taking place which can help you to either take advantage of a positive development or minimize any risk in the case of a negative one. This information will also help you to understand what kind of returns you can expect from any potential properties so that you can strategize accordingly.

Whenever you plan to invest in a buy to let, you have to ask yourself which locations or property types you can expect the highest rental income from, and who the target consumers in a particular town or area are. Once you have your initial target consumers—or tenants—in mind, you can then seek out the best kind of property that will attract your ideal tenant, while also measuring the property's potential rental yield. Based on the advice and information you get from the market, you can then determine the right time to acquire a new property as well as when the best time to sell an existing property for a handsome profit will be. Always be ready to make more connections in the property business, such as meeting with other landlords, solicitors, accountants, estate agents, and investors. You will find that a lot of other people in the market are likely in a similar boat as you, and they are abuzz with information and tidbits that help each other out of any kind of pickle.

Also, do not overexert yourself. Going into a business idea with all guns blazing can spread you out too thin and make you lose sight of your goals. You might think that making multiple investments in a diverse property portfolio will lead you to immediate results, but this is something that should be done slowly and one step, or property, at a time. Start with one or two buy to let properties so that you gain the necessary knowledge, experience, and confidence to acquire a third, then a fourth, and then more properties. No investment is problem-free, which is why it is important to minimize the risk by experiencing issues in one or two investments instead of five or six simultaneously. The more you expand yourself from the get-go, the higher the chances are of making mistakes if all you do is acquire and forget to properly manage.

It is also a great idea to try specializing in one particular kind of buy to let property first before thinking of diversifying. Oftentimes, you will hear divided opinions on committing fully to either specializing or diversifying, but there are advantages and disadvantages to both approaches. If you specialize in one type of property, you benefit from gaining considerable experience in the niche and also develop great rapport with a particular type of client or tenant. This way, you master one arena and learn to make fewer mistakes. But like putting your eggs in one basket, you hedge your bets on one particular investment while overlooking the advantages of another type of property. If there is an unfortunate downturn in your specialized property market, you risk losing out on potential rental income and any profit on the property value if the market goes down. A recent example of this is all the student lets that were vacated during the COVID-19 pandemic, as students were forced to return to their hometowns.

On the other hand, you can spread out the risk on different types of properties by diversifying your portfolio so that the changing circumstances on one kind of property can be offset by the growth in another. If the property market is doing well as a whole, you stand to make a windfall in rental income and grow your business so that you can leverage it further. The only drawback is that you will have a lot to learn about multiple property types and the various dynamics of how those markets work; most important of which is developing rapport with all kinds of tenants. Though this is a welcome chance for you to gain considerable experience in a diverse market, you will find that you may not be well-suited for a certain kind of tenant or market, which could negatively affect how you treat your entire portfolio.

This brings up another valuable point: being a great landlord. Customer satisfaction is an essential component in any business, and buy to let consumers have their own metrics with which they measure satisfaction. This isn't a retail business or a phone service provider that they can change up if they do not feel happy. This is a long-term commitment about where they live, how they spend a great deal of their time, and what kind of quality of life they will lead. Don't forget that they are paying you a sizable portion of their income, or their parents are if they are students, for a habitable and comfortable lifestyle, so you have to deliver to the best of your abilities and give them their money's worth. This means resolving any maintenance issues at the earliest possible convenience, being available in case of any unforeseen accidents or incidents such as a burglary or invasion of privacy, offering safe, secure, and quality accommodation with the proper certifications, ensuring rapid communication, and contributing to communal space. Aside from that, be sure that all your legal obligations to your tenants are fulfilled.

How well you accommodate them and show flexibility will increase their level of satisfaction, and motivate them to become great and responsible tenants. They will become invested in your property and take care of it even though they are only there for a certain period of time, and also ensure that there is no bad blood with delayed rents. That said, you should also do your due diligence by identifying your potential tenants and weeding out any problematic ones who won't be doing your business and assets any good. If you notice anything shaky about their background or financial position, you should minimize that risk factor immediately. This way, you avoid any periods where your property is vacated, which could result in a loss of revenue.

Cover Any Pitfalls

One area that landlords and buyers often overlook is the benefit of investing locally. While investing in a commuter town or near a university sounds ideal if you want to attract a pool of readily-available tenants, and also benefit from lower property prices than you would get in The City, it becomes a hassle if you live away from that town. You will then have to hire a letting agent to be a property manager if you are unable to handle the responsibilities yourself, which adds on to your cost and depletes your Positive Cash Flow.

Instead, invest in local buy to lets. This will help you polish your skills as a landlord, and allow you to be more hands-on with all aspects of managing the property and looking after your tenants. Tenants will also be assured that you will be personally available to handle any issues with maintenance, while also being aware of your local council and authority requirements. Furthermore, you know the lay of the land, so you can seek out relevant contractors, estate agents, accountants, and other service providers without having to deal with someone new. This way, you can get the best price for any work or service required. You will get an idea of how much it costs to do things in your location so that you can have a better idea of what to compare with once you set your eyes on expanding out of your hometown.

On the other hand, hiring a letting agent could become necessary once your portfolio expands outwards into the rest of the country. Since you cannot be expected to be too hands-on and will have a wider scope of properties to manage, a letting agent can take on the responsibility of managing the property on your behalf for the right price. By then, however, your profit margins should allow you to hire one, as it can provide you with a great deal of benefits when expanding in another town or city. For one thing, they will have greater insights into the kind of tenants in another town and how those tenants can be evaluated for your property. For another thing, they can be more hands-on in a particular town and ensure faster service turnaround time if tenants face any issues.

There is no problem in delegating these matters to a letting agent as long as your Positive Cash Flow can afford it. This will allow you more time to manage the rest of your assets and strategize how you want to grow. Don't forget that being a hands-on landlord is a full-time job and you cannot be expected to travel to different towns and cities whenever a tenant reports a faulty boiler. While the goal is to make passive income, you should remember that it has to be carried out sensibly and responsibly.

It is also a great idea to own your properties under a limited company. This will offer you many tax advantages versus if you owned the properties in your own name, as reviewed in Chapter 5 of this book. Also, your personal property is also protected in the event your buy to let property portfolio suffers any setbacks. Nevertheless, you should carefully go through all the pros and cons of a limited company by getting necessary advice from a qualified accountant.

You should also be careful not to make a greater offer than what the property is likely worth. Instead, be prepared to ask considerably lower than the market selling price. At worst, the seller will say no, but at best, the seller may be ready to negotiate and meet you halfway to an acceptable price. If you are ready to pay the exact asking price, or even overpay if you find a great property, your profit margins will take a hit which can be easily prevented. Look for an ideal time to invest in a new property when the prices suit your budget. This is where keeping abreast of the market trends is necessary.

Another thing to avoid is cross-collateralization. This happens when you mortgage against the value of several properties at the same time if you feel that you can grow a lot more rapidly than you should be. Oftentimes, you will come across very lucrative and potentially no-fail properties that would make for sound investments, but if this happens quite frequently, you end up having more mortgaged properties than you can handle. What that does is create a domino effect, wherein the loss on one investment could result in all of your other investments coming under risk. If one investment turns sour, you will need to sell multiple properties just to avoid going into debt. It's akin to using one credit card to settle the debt of another credit card and so on, wherein you are paying off for a property with money you do not have. Take property investing as a marathon where you have to perform consistently and slowly gain an advantage—or find your advantage—instead of taking it as a spring and exhausting yourself from the get-go. Think years and decades rather than months when it comes to the buy to let portfolio game.

Eventually, like most other businesses, you will reach a point where you finally cash out and retire. Perhaps you want to move on and live a life with all your massive profits, or perhaps you feel that you have achieved all you could in your investments. In any event, you should consider having an exit strategy so that you can leave a healthy and profitable buy to let business portfolio to the next potential investor and also make a fortune out of your profits once you retire. You should look for the right time when the property market hits a high and be prepared to sell up when you notice that the market is doing well and will attract potential investors to your business.

Conclusion

No matter what the condition of the market plays, whether good or bad, investing in buy to lets can provide you with significant returns if you play your cards right. Every single bit of research you do in the beginning is aimed at helping you find the most ideal property with the best option for you to finance it if you don't have the capital at hand. Mortgaging is a necessary step for hopping on to the property train, which is why, throughout this book, we have reviewed how important it is to get the best advice from people who are more in-tune with how the market works. Whether it is an accountant who has their own investments in buy to let properties, estate agents who are looking to pair the best tenants with the best landlords and properties, mortgage brokers who can bring you the best financing deals available, or legal representatives who ensure you are fulfilling all your obligations according to the rules and regulations, you need to act sensibly and solicit help from all quarters. Doing it all alone can not just be daunting, but also stressful and time consuming with every chance of slip-ups along the way if you stretch yourself too thin.

Of course, your involvement in the whole business is essential. Without your oversight and instruction, your team of experts won't be able to give you the best advice and offer you the best deals on the market. Nevertheless, your goal as a buy to let property investor should be to look at the big picture and how to make the properties—and your people—work for you. Naturally, you will need to roll up your sleeves and get into the thick of it when you are starting out, as being a hands-on landlord will require you to be present and ready to assist your tenants whenever needed. But you have to visualize where you see yourself and your business years down the line and bring all your experiences, resources, and people together to achieve your goal of creating passive wealth and expanding your property holdings in order to maximize your cash inflows.

Remember where you are at present and where you see yourself in 10 years time as you cash out your profits and wealth and decide to retire. Once you have the starting and finishing points set up, you simply need to fill in the gaps with the necessary steps to take in order to get to that finish line. This will involve short, long, and even medium-term investment strategies and a sharp lookout for opportunities, pitfalls, and the way the market winds are blowing so that you can make sensible decisions and grow your business over time.

I hope that you enjoyed reading *Build Your Wealth Through Property Investment: The Essential Buy to Let Property Investment Strategies for UK Investors* and would love to hear from you on Amazon. To learn more on how you can create a valuable business model in the UK property sector, do check out *Build Your Wealth Through Property Investments: Dissecting the 8 Most Popular Types of UK Property Investment Strategies,* also available on Amazon.

References

Bedford, D. (n.d.). *Buying a flat with a short lease: What you need to know*. Www.pettyson.co.uk. Retrieved December 31, 2022, from https://www.pettyson.co.uk/about-us/our-blog/561-buying-a-flat-with-a-short-lease

Beecham, W. (2022, June 20). *Buying your first buy-to-let investment property*. Progressive Lets. https://www.progressivelets.co.uk/landlords/buying-your-first-buy-to-let-btl-investment-property/

Central Bank of Ireland. (n.d.). *Explainer - What is the tracker mortgage examination?* Central Bank of Ireland. Retrieved December 17, 2022, from https://www.centralbank.ie/consumer-hub/explainers/what-is-the-tracker-mortgage-examination

Clifton Private Finance. (2020, November 24). *How to get refurbishment finance for a buy to let property*. Www.cliftonpf.co.uk. https://www.cliftonpf.co.uk/blog/11052017094219-how-to-get-refurbishment-finance-for-a-buy-to-let-property/#

CloudCo Accountants. (2022, May 10). *How to avoid capital gains tax on buy-to-let property*. CloudCo Accountants. https://cloudcogroup.com/how-to-avoid-capital-gains-tax-on-buy-to-let-property/

Cox, H. (2021, February 19). *London landlords feel the burden of buy-to-lets*. Financial Times. https://www.ft.com/content/cd12e80d-927b-4024-bf9c-49ee0fd7c042

Equifax. (n.d.). *What is a tracker mortgage?*. Equifax UK. Retrieved December 17, 2022, from https://www.equifax.co.uk/resources/mortgage/tracker-mortgages.html

Fay, S. (2011, August 1). *Top 10 questions to ask when choosing an accountant*. Fylde Tax Accountants. https://www.fyldetaxaccountants.co.uk/property-articles/top-10-questions-ask-choosing-accountant/

Gov.UK. (n.d.). *House in multiple occupation licence*. Gov.UK. https://www.gov.uk/house-in-multiple-occupation-licence

Government Digital Service. (2011, November 9). *Housing association homes*. GOV.UK. https://www.gov.uk/housing-association-homes/types-of-tenancy

Herts Advertiser. (2020, March 22). *Sunday Times names St Albans as one of UK's best places to live*. Herts Advertiser. https://www.hertsad.co.uk/lifestyle/21793021.sunday-times-names-st-albans-one-uks-best-places-live/

HomeLet. (n.d.). *Responsibility of tenants of furnished accommodation*. HomeLet. Retrieved December 25, 2022, from https://homelet.co.uk/tenants/tips-for-tenants/responsibility-of-tenants-of-furnished-accommodation

HomeOwners Alliance. (n.d.-a). *Government schemes to help you buy a home*. HomeOwners Alliance. https://hoa.org.uk/advice/guides-for-homeowners/i-am-buying/government-schemes-help-buy-home/

HomeOwners Alliance. (n.d.-a). *Help To Buy equity loan 2021-2023*. HomeOwners Alliance. https://hoa.org.uk/advice/guides-for-homeowners/i-am-buying/help-to-buy/

HomeOwners Alliance. (n.d.). *New build vs existing home - The pros and cons*. HomeOwners Alliance. https://hoa.org.uk/advice/guides-for-homeowners/i-am-buying/new-build-vs-existing-home/

HomeOwners Alliance. (2016). *New home warranties - What they do and don't cover*. HomeOwners Alliance. https://hoa.org.uk/advice/guides-for-homeowners/i-am-buying/new-home-warranties-cover/

HomeOwners Alliance. (2022, January 4). *How much does an EPC cost?*. HomeOwners Alliance. https://hoa.org.uk/advice/guides-for-homeowners/i-am-selling/how-much-does-an-epc-cost/

Horne, B. (2019, February 10). *Revealed: 16 homes to avoid if you want to get a mortgage*. Which? News. https://www.which.co.uk/news/article/revealed-16-homes-to-avoid-if-you-want-to-get-a-mortgage-a4Q6O3T5i5Ov

Jenkin, M. (2022, November 24). *Buying a house or flat in London*. Which? News. https://www.which.co.uk/money/mortgages-and-property/buying-a-home/buying-a-house-or-flat-in-london-aJLfe3p12JiA

Jessel, E. (2022, April 11). *What does the buy-to-let bounce mean for London renters?* Evening Standard. https://www.standard.co.uk/homesandproperty/renting/buytolet-increase-london-renters-b993351.html

Leaders. (2019, August 21). *Buying property for renovation- Pros and cons.* Leaders. https://www.leaders.co.uk/advice/buying-property-to-renovate

Lewis, C. (2022, May 18). *UK House Price Index.* Office for National Statistics. https://www.ons.gov.uk/economy/inflationandpriceindices/bulletins/housepriceindex/march2022

Lockings. (2021, December 22). *What is a conveyancing solicitor, and what do they do?* Lockings Solicitors. https://www.lockings.co.uk/what-is-a-conveyancing-solicitor/

Magenis, I. (2021, September 24). *The guide to buy-to-let property management.* Scanlans Property Management. https://www.scanlanspropertymanagement.com/the-guide-to-buy-to-let-property-management/

Market Business News. (n.d.). *White goods - definition and meaning.* Market Business News. https://marketbusinessnews.com/financial-glossary/white-goods-definition-meaning/

Market Financial Solutions. (2021, July 29). *The best London commuter towns: Opportunities near the city.* Market Financial Solutions. https://www.mfsuk.com/blog/mfs-top-5-commuter-towns/

Market Financial Solutions. (2022a). *The homebuyer wishlist*. Market Financial Solutions. https://www.mfsuk.com/wp-content/uploads/2022/03/The-Homebuyer-Wishlist.pdf

Market Financial Solutions. (2022b, June 13). *What is buy-to-let property & things to consider before investing*. Market Financial Solutions. https://www.mfsuk.com/blog/what-is-a-buy-to-let-investment/

Office for National Statistics. (2021, July 14). *Index of private housing rental prices, UK*. Office for National Statistics. https://www.ons.gov.uk/economy/inflationandpriceindices/bulletins/indexofprivatehousingrentalprices/june2021

Otte, J. (2022, May 11). *Nine buy-to-let tips for beginners*. The Times. https://www.thetimes.co.uk/money-mentor/article/buy-to-let-tips/

Parkers Properties. (2021, May 4). *Six Things to consider when buying a property to renovate*. Parkers. https://www.parkersproperties.co.uk/news/buying-house-that-needs-renovation

Punjwani, M. (2019, March 7). *Choosing the right buy-to-let property*. MoneySuperMarket. https://www.moneysupermarket.com/landlord-insurance/choosing-buy-to-let-properties/

reallymoving. (n.d.). *Purchasing buy to let property: 11 top tips*. Reallymoving. Retrieved December 26, 2022, from https://www.reallymoving.com/conveyancing/guides/purchasing-buy-to-let-property-11-top-tips

Rightmove PLC. (2009, July 31). *House Price Index*. Rightmove. https://www.rightmove.co.uk/news/house-price-index/

Shelter England. (2022, February 24). *Electrical safety in rented homes*. Shelter England. https://england.shelter.org.uk/housing_advice/repairs/electrical_safety_in_rented_homes

Statista. (2022, February 2). *Age profile of tenure groups England 2020*. Statista. https://www.statista.com/statistics/286451/england-age-characteristics-of-household-tenure-groups/

Uberoi, R. (2022, April 4). *Investment buy to let property in London*. Starck Uberoi Solicitors. https://www.starckuberoi.co.uk/investment-buy-to-let-property-london/

UK Landlord Tax. (2020). *What is the landlord licensing scheme?* UKLandlordTax. https://uklandlordtax.co.uk/advice/legal/what-is-the-landlord-licensing-scheme/

United Nations. (2021, September 3). *Air quality improvements from COVID lockdowns confirmed*. UN News. https://news.un.org/en/story/2021/09/1099092

Upad. (n.d.). *How do you choose the right buy to let investment?* Upad. Retrieved December 28, 2022, from https://www.upad.co.uk/hub/essential-tips/how-to-maximise-your-rental-income/how-do-you-choose-the-right-buy-to-let-investment

Zoopla. (n.d.). *House prices in Stalbans - sold prices and estimates.* Zoopla. https://www.zoopla.co.uk/house-prices/stalbans/